Secrets from New York's (Best) Restaurants

EARLYNE S. LEVITAS
&
LYDIA MOSS

Secrets from New York's (Best) Restaurants

Original Illustrations:
Ed Allgor, Laurie Engel, and Barbara Glick

Published by

Secrets

Post Office Box 10252
Atlanta, Georgia 30319

BOOKS BY EARLYNE S. LEVITAS

Secrets from New York's Best Restaurants
(with **LYDIA MOSS**)

Secrets from Atlanta's Best Kitchens
Secrets from New Orleans' Best Kitchens
Secrets from the South's Best Restaurants

Over 100,000 Secrets now in print

First Printing — February 1975
Second Printing — September 1975

TO OUR HUSBANDS
TED AND STEVE

Perhaps the greatest gourmand who ever lived, Jean Anthelme Brillat-Savarin once said, "The discovery of a new dish does more for the happiness of mankind than the discovery of a new star." We feel in discovering a great restaurant, you experience one of the most sensuous pleasures in the world. We love restaurants!

To report on the best or most loved restaurants in a city as enormous as New York takes years and years of dining out. This we have done. In attempting this awesome and calorie consuming task, we followed a familiar pattern . . . the one that has proved so successful in writing three previous books . . . "Secrets from Atlanta's Best Kitchens", "Secrets from New Orleans' Best Kitchens", and "Secrets from the South's Best Restaurants".

In judging the hundreds of restaurants we visited, we tried to chose those that best lived up to our standards of consistency, imaginative preparation, originality, and courteous service. Numerous food critics race around the city rating the New York restaurants on a dozen different slide rules. We do not agree completely with any of them.

This book is meant to serve a twofold purpose . . . as a guidebook to some of the finest dining in the country and a means of reproducing these famous dishes in your own kitchen. Many of the fantastic dishes are relatively easy to prepare at home. Enjoy yourself and happy cooking!

New York has always been the giant melting pot of America, and we have peeked into nearly all the kitchens you will read about. This unique city is the epicurean capital of America, and from the thousands of little ethnic restaurants, came some of the most interesting dishes we discovered.

We are grateful to the many restaurateurs of the city who showed us kindness, consideration, and often tried to extend hospitality while we were in the process of writing. It has been our firm policy to accept no free meals - or to announce our presence or intent on the first visit. The intensity of our work can be best summed up in an outline of a typical day. There was that hot summer day when we had lunch at the Four Season's cooking school, a second lunch at the 21 Club, and at 2:30 in the afternoon, we were nibbling with the chef at the Swiss Pavillion. By 5:30 we were cutting into a gigantic steak at The Palm, and smacking our lips in approval. It plays havoc with the waistline and any normal schedule to tackle the restaurants of a giant city, but we both feel that the experience was fantastic.

Most chefs would rather part with a pint of their blood than a recipe, but with all the charms we could muster up, we never had to take no for an answer. Everytime a restaurateur or chef gave us a new recipe, we were like delighted children . . . so pleased to add another coup to this book for our readers to share.

The art of superb cooking is usually a tedious road. Many of the most famous chefs started their apprenticeships in Europe and worked their way up from one restaurant to another. We are now blessed to count dozens of interesting new people on our list of talented friends . . . most of them work 14 to 16 hours a day and manage to keep a sense of humor and delightful philosophy. Our hats off to these wonderful men in the tall white hats . . . and to our readers, Bon Appetit!

Earlyne S. Levitas and Lydia Moss

Contents

La Caravelle

One of the greatest chefs in the history of New York restaurants, Charles Ranhofer, long ago said, "The culinary art may be the distinguishing thing of civilization, and in its perfection, it is the inspiration of genius . . ." The masterful finesse of New York's marvelous La Caravelle is the inspiration of two geniuses . . . Owners Fred Decre' and Robert Meyzen.

Since 1960, this great French restaurant has come as close to perfection as any restaurant in America, and its consistency has been a source of delight to knowledgeable diners from around the world. Enter the cool, sedate private world of Caravelle through a dignified entrance on 55th Street. Here you find a restaurant that sails smoothly like the ancient caravels . . . the motto and logo of the restaurant. There is great elegance in the simplicity of muted pastel colors, soft velvets, intimate seating, and murals of Paris street scenes painted by Jean Pages. In this quiet atmosphere, soft voices are mingled with superb service, while a powerful kitchen is in motion producing chicken in champagne sauce, turbot, stuffed artichokes, magnificent desserts and exquisite dishes that rarely meet diners in the country.

A crescent shaped bar, hidden from view, is a wisp of a stop before being seated. My favorite Kir is a lovely beginning for the gourmet treat you are about to enjoy. Chilled white wine is laced with a few drops of Creme of Cassis. There is hardly a nicer apertif in the world and it is a perfect complement to the incredible feast at La Caravelle.

Just as the old traditional French kitchens of Europe, the famous kitchen at Caravelle is finished in faded oak wall coverings, old-fashioned utensils and an abundance of beautifully fresh fruits and vegetables that are a spectacle to behold! From all over the world come these magnificent ingredients to pamper your palate.

A large French menu is intriguing; it is like reading a culinary list of the finest of classic French cuisine. Between mouthwatering thoughts, your eye catches a glimpse of the impressive guests arriving. Society matrons stroll in with floppy hats, Kenneth coiffures, Bonwit fashions, evenly capped smiles, and handsome escorts. There is a prix fixe menu each evening for under $20 and a notable luncheon offered at $12.75. Many luncheon items are fantastic, making this an extremely popular place for lunch in Manhattan. It is a breathtaking experience and should be enjoyed in leisure.

Appetizers are exciting and imaginative. Crabmeat Gribiche, served on an oversized artichoke heart, Mousse de Brochet Havraise, an elegant loaf prepared with pike and shrimp, Gratin de Fruits de Mer, a creamy blend of lobster, crabmeat and scallops, are just a few of the daily specials that entice gourmands. This is haute everything!

It is an impossibility to single out the greatest dish, so you will come back many times to sample the excellence of this brilliant kitchen. Roger Fessaguet, the magnificent chef at Caravelle, presides in his whites over a staff that starts the working day at 7 a. m. Saute de Caneton au Poivre, saddle of rare lamb, Sole Doria and Le Bass Grenoublaise are just a few of the memorable entrees. The duck is perhaps the finest known to man . . . crisp, golden, and served with a spectacular sour cream sauce.

Whether it is a rare fresh vegetable from Nigeria or turbot from France, there is no limit in Caravelle's constant search for the finest food and wine that can be bought. I am not the first writer to be amazed at

4

the wonderful, reasonably priced wines. The wine list ranges from moderate priced wines to some of the rarest vintages bottled.

The demanding palate, created by world travel, and the wide interest in wines in this country have contributed to the large number of businessmen who arrive around 1:30 each day. Many business deals are quietly discussed while nibbling Foie Gras, Quail eggs, and Beluga Caviar.

Desserts are memorable. There is an endless array of gorgeous fruit pastries, Napoleons, flaming dishes, souffles, as well as a Chocolate Mousse that reigns supreme. Prepared with great expertise by one of the dessert chefs, it is wicked, sinful, and wonderful. Raspberries Romanoff are particularly delicious after a heavy meal. Gigantic, plump red berries float in a dreamy, light sauce.

From the subtle sauces to the not so subtle Expresso, you will receive the finest quality food, beautifully served, and an indulgence that is almost divine. Good taste seems innate in every aspect of this four star restaurant and there is pure pleasure in one of the most gargantuan dinners found in America.

Treat yourself to a memorable evening. Call for reservations and visit Caravelle. Evening finds congenial groups of genteel diners, gracious exchange of conversation, appreciative questions and comments. As guests slowly fill the banquettes, the chef is like a great maestro . . . ready to burst into song with his well trained staff. Everything begins to hummm . . . great wines begin to chill, wire whisks begin to stir, menus appear, and after a full day's work, the moment of glory is here.

All these glorious things don't just happen. The success of any restaurant is no greater than the owner. A recent issue of Bazaar described Mr. Meyzen

5

as "jolly, moustached, every inch the prosperous Frenchman in his well-cut dark blue suit." It continued in describing Mr. Decre' . . . "he has the looks of a Zurich banker and a wit as dry as Chablis." With two such charming owners, how could Caravelle be less than fantastic?

For their dedication and skill, for the consistent magnificence in cuisine, for the beauty of fine service and great wines, I salute the owners of La Caravelle . . . Fred Decre' and Robert Meyzen. They are worthy of all the poetic lines that have praised their talents. May the Caravelle continue sailing with smoothness. Bon voyage and Bon Appetit!!

Canapes de Saumon

from La Caravelle

¼ pound freshly poached salmon

Few sprigs of parsley, minced

Big pinch of minced chives

2 shallots, peeled and minced

3 tsp. mayonnaise

1 hard boiled egg, chopped fine

Salt

Freshly ground white pepper

Flake the salmon, then combine with the remaining ingredients. Add salt and pepper. Spread on rounds of toasted white bread. Garnish with sliced stuffed olives or little diamonds of black truffle.

Makes 18 canapes.

Canard Smitane

from La Caravelle

1 duckling
Salt
Freshly ground pepper
½ small yellow onion,
peeled and minced

1 stick butter
1/3 cup wine vinegar
1/3 cup dry white wine
1 cup heavy cream

Pull any lumps of fat from the cavity and neck of the duck. Salt and pepper inside and out. Truss. To help the duck release surplus fat, prick the skin along the thighs and back. Place on the rack of a roasting pan, breast side up and roast for about an hour in a hot oven. (400 degrees.) The legs should feel soft when pierced with a fork.

Lift the duck from the pan and remove the trussing strings. Put on a serving platter and keep warm in a low oven. Pour all the fat off the pan and add half the butter and the onion. Cook over medium heat, stirring in all the drippings and crust that clings to the pan. When the onion is lightly browned, add the vinegar and wine. Bring to a boil and reduce to about one third. Stir in the cream and reduce to about three fourths. Add salt and pepper and remaining butter. Strain through a sieve into a sauceboat and serve with rice.

Serves 2.

Red Snapper a L'Espagnole

from La Caravelle

1 red snapper (3 to 4 pounds), cleaned head left on.
Salt and pepper
1 tsp. leaf thyme, crumbled
2 bay leaves
Saffron
8 to 10 garlic cloves, finely chopped
1 cup diced onion
2 small green peppers, chopped

7 tomatoes, peeled, seeded and chopped
4 T. olive oil
2 cups Fish Fumet (directions included)
2 cups dry white wine
3 medium potatoes, diced and blanched in boiling water 1 minute
Chopped parsley

Wash fish and pat dry. Season with salt and pepper. Place in a large oiled roasting pan and sprinkle inside with thyme, bay leaves, pinch of saffron, and 1 tsp. of the garlic. Close cavity with skewers.

Saute' onion and green pepper. Cook for about five minutes in a skillet with a small amount of hot oil. Add the remainder of the garlic and saute' another two minutes. Stir in tomatoes. Cook 10 to 15 minutes. Add potatoes.

Spoon vegetable mixture over and around the fish. Pour in fish fumet and wine. Put pan directly over heat and bring to a boil. Cover with foil. Bake in a 375 degree oven for about 30 minutes. Transfer fish to deep platter. Set roasting pan over heat and boil mixture until it is reduced to one half in volume. Spoon sauce

8

and vegetables over the fish. Sprinkle with fresh parsley. Serves 8 appetizers.

Fond Blanc or White Stock

from La Caravelle

This stock may be cooked and stored in the freezer.

3 pounds meaty veal shank, sawed into small pieces

1 pound chicken wings, necks and backs

3 quarts cold water

1 onion, quartered

1 carrot cut into one-inch pieces

1 leek, chopped coarsely

5 sprigs parsley

¼ tsp. leaf thyme, crumbled

1 bay leaf

6 peppercorns

1 tsp. salt

Combine veal, chicken and water in soup kettle. Bring to a boil, skimming the foam off the top. Lower heat and simmer for 30 minutes. Add onion, carrot celery, leek, parsley, thyme, bay leaf, peppercorns and salt. Cover kettle and simmer for three hours.

Strain broth through a double thickness of cheese cloth into a large bowl. Cool, then chill or freeze.

Fish Fumet (Basic Fish Stock)

from La Caravelle

1 medium onion, sliced

6 sprigs parsley

½ tsp. salt

1 pound fish bones

3½ cups water

½ cup dry white wine

2 T. lemon juice

Place onion, parsley, salt and the bones in a large saucepan. Add water, wine, and lemon juice. Bring to a boil. Reduce heat and simmer 30 minutes. Strain through a cheesecloth.

Discard bones and vegetables. Boil broth until it is reduced to about two cups.

Canapes de Goelands

from La Caravelle

1 4⅜ can imported boneless sardines, drained

2 shallots, peeled and minced

3 sprigs parsley, minced

1 Tbsp. wine vinegar

Salt

Freshly ground pepper

With a fork, blend the ingredients together. Spread on toasted white bread triangles.

Makes 16 Canapes.

Apple Tart a la Tatin

from La Caravelle

4 pounds Rome Beauty apples
1 stick sweet butter
2 cups sugar
Baking dish 10 inches in diameter

Combine the butter and sugar in a saucepan and cook until it is a "blond" caramel. Remove from the heat and cool. Pour into the baking dish.

Peel, core and quarter the apples. Arrange on top of the caramel and place in a preheated 450 degree oven for 45 minutes.

Pastry:

2 cups all-purpose flour
pinch salt
1 Tbsp. sugar
1 stick sweet butter
5 Tbsp. ice water

Place half of the flour in a bowl and stir in the salt and sugar. Add the butter that has been cut into pieces. Work with a pastry blender until the fat is broken into pieces the size of a pea. Work in the remaining flour. Finally, sprinkle the dough with water and shape it into a ball. Wrap in waxed paper and refrigerate for a few hours.

Roll the pastry into a circle smaller than the diameter of the dish. Roll over the pin and center over the pie dish. Return to the oven and continue baking another 15 minutes or until the crust is golden. Cool for a few minutes. Serve lukewarm.

Serves 6.

11

The Coach House

Back in the '40's a diligent young man from Corfu arrived in New York to study engineering. While a student he often lunched at Helen Lanes, a ladies' tea room housed in a delightful old carriage house a few hundred feet from Washington Square. So enamored was he by this restaurant that the man, Leon Leonides, was soon telling friends that some day he would buy this old house. He did. He also switched professions. In time the simple tea room, much like Cinderella, was transformed into the beautiful Coach House.

People often say that an elegant American restaurant is hard to find in New York. Those who have discovered the Coach House know differently. Think of New York in the 19th century . . . back to the days of Henry James' Washington Square. Picture horse drawn carriages moving slowly along still unpaved streets. A bit of this era is preserved at the Coach House where gas lamps still flicker lighting up the brick facade and welcoming diners to this 1850 landmark house.

The dining room abounds with charm. Brick and wood paneled walls . . . old copper pots . . . lovely coach lamps add to the dining mood here. Upstairs, a quiet dining room has replaced what was once a hayloft.

Originally the house was a stable on the Wanamaker estate in what was then a most fashionable part of town. Today, sophisticated diners frequent this special restaurant. Many, who have graced the comfortable red banquettes are well known and famous. Visiting French chef Troisgros was captivated by the black bean soup and pepper steak. He left with the recipe for the famed corn bread sticks. When Aristotle Onassis dined here he too, carried something off with him . . . a bag full of sausage and lentil salad.

13

What is it about the Coach House draws demanding diners from all over the world? Owner Leonides is demanding himself and over the years has run a consistant and almost flawless kitchen. From the delicious hot cornsticks brought to the table warm from the oven to the unbelievably tasty pecan pie smothered with freshly whipped cream (both coincidentally holdovers from the tea room days) your dinner will be a memorable one.

Praise has come from near and far. Craig Clairborne, the dean of New York food writers, has referred to The Coach House as his favorite New York Restaurant. Dishes here consistantly live up to their reputation. American specialties are outstanding. Exquisite and tender roast prime ribs of beef have long been the house favorite. The rack of lamb is perfectly roasted and piqued with fresh garden herbs. Continental and Greek dishes reflect Leonides' boyhood days in Greece and his studies at L'Ecole des Trois Gourmandes in Paris. Chef Raoul Santana who hails from the southern part of the United States brings another dimension to the cuisine.

Most regulars prefer to start with the famed black bean soup, flavored with a touch of Madeira. I can hardly blame them. But I also enjoy the hors d'oeuvres varies. This selection of several appetizers . . . fresh mushrooms a la Greque, eggplant provencale, pate maison and herring in cream sauce is practically a meal in itself.

Well deserving of the raves they receive are the enormous triple cut lamb chops. Also noteworthy are the mignonettes of veal dressed with glazed chestnuts and a delicate striped bass poached in fresh tomatoes and white wine. Seasonal specialties might include sauteed soft shell crabs or venison stew.

Cassoulet is prepared occasionally at lunch and fans

of this dish phone in to find out when it's being served. James Beard once investigated cassoulets available in the city and described the one served at the Coach House as the most peasant-like and strikingly different of all the cassoulets he sampled.

Nothing at the Coach House quite matches up to the devastating dessert table. The legendary chocolate cake has a candy-like chocolate filling that is second to none. I have made it at home for everything from campaign parties to barbeques, with never even a crumb remaining. Other after meal masterpieces not to be overlooked are dacoise . . . a sweet and delicious French concoction of meringue and butter cream . . . bread and butter pudding and fresh fruit tarts.

You can visit The Coach House every day except Monday. Only dinner is served on Saturday and Sunday. It's expensive. Dinner for two with a good American wine will run about $60.

No one should ever have to rush through a meal here so come prepared to spend several hours and enjoy a leisurely dinner. I mentioned earlier that Leonides is demanding. One demand that he makes upon guests is that they have a reservation.

While it is located in Greenwich Village where informality generally prevails, The Coach House is unlike the neighboring restaurants, or any other in town for that matter. Thanks to Mr. Leonides it has come a long way since those early tea room days. It is first class dining . . . it is elegance all the way . . . and it should not be missed.

Black Bean Soup

from The Coach House

4 cups black beans
5 quarts cold water
½ cup butter
3 stalks of celery
3 large onions, chopped
2½ T. flour
½ cup finely chopped
  parsley
3 leeks, thinly sliced
4 bay leaves

1 T. salt
½ tsp. freshly ground
  pepper
Bone and rind of a cooked
  smoked ham (or 1
  pound smoked pork
  knuckles)
1 cup dry Madeira
  wine
2 hard-cooked eggs,
  finely chopped
2 lemons, thinly sliced

Pick over and wash black beans, and soak over night in cold water to cover. Drain beans and place them in a large kettle with water. Bring to boil. Cook slowly over low heat for 1½ hours.

Melt the butter in a saucepan and saute' the celery and onions for 10 minutes. Stir in the flour and parsley, continuing to cook and stir for a few minutes. Add the mixture to the beans, along with the ham bone, leeks, bay leaves, and salt and pepper. Simmer for 3 hours.

Remove and discard the bones and bay leaves. Force beans through a seive or food grinder. Return the beans and broth to the kettle. Add dry Madeira wine. Heat the soup and remove from stove. Stir in the hard-cooked eggs. Float a thin slice of lemon on each serving.

Corn Bread

from The Coach House

1 cup all-purpose flour
1 cup water-ground
  cornmeal
4 tsp. baking powder
2 Tbsp. sugar

1 tsp. salt
1½ cups milk
2 eggs, beaten
¼ cup butter, melted

Sift together the flour, cornmeal, baking powder, sugar, and salt. Combine the milk and eggs and stir into the dry ingredients. Add the melted butter. Stir quickly, just until it is well blended. Pour the batter into a lightly greased round cake pan.

Bake in a preheated oven set at 425 degrees for 30 minutes or until golden brown. May be baked in corn stick molds.

Makes 1 9-inch loaf.

La Cote Basque

Still dominating the restaurant scene in New York is the legend and memory of one of the greatest gourmands who ever lived. This genius of a man, Henri Soule, earned the lofty reputation as "the greatest restaurateur in the world" and added a new dimension to American dining. He was an unpretentious man, but his accomplishments were masterful.

In the late 1950's, Henri Soule was enjoying an unprecedented success in his world-famous restaurant, Le Pavillon. His kitchen was the training ground for hundreds of chefs, waiters, and auxilliary restaurant personnel, and they learned the grand art of preparing and serving the loveliest cuisine known to man. With all the success of Pavillon at a peak, Mr. Soule opened a second restaurant . . . serving many of the same exquisite French specialties, but the meals were less expensive. He labeled his new offspring . . . La Cote Basque, and today it is considered to be one of the most exceptional restaurants in America.

Just off Fifth Avenue you may join the world of interesting diners who assemble at 5 E. 55th Street for fabulous lunches and dinners. The great name of the late owner still lingers on the waving canopy, and the same glorious dishes stream from the famous kitchen.

Step into the large, colorful dining room, and you will feel that you have left Manhattan. Murals, painted by Bernard Lamotte, give the distinct impression that you are dining in a secluded village in France. Heavy dark beams line the ceilings and soft red velvets line the banquettes. It is a wonderful combination of effects.

What sensual pleasures . . . wine . . . flowers . . . exceptional foods . . . purposeful people forgetting their purpose and enjoying life . . . that quality of individuality and greatness that gives a restaurant its own unique personality.

19

Amidst the excitement of cheerful guests arriving for lunch, the bar opens for its first pourings of the day. Have something light, perhaps a Kir, for the best is yet to come. An air of festivity is created by the abundance of fresh flowers. There is also a special delight in the courteous and attentive waiters who do an excellent job.

Cold appetizers before lunch is an ongoing French tradition, and after you have sampled a delicacy such as cold striped bass, offered with green sauce or sauce gribiche, you will understand why French cuisine and recipes are cherished the world over! Nibble delicious marinated artichokes, tangy with a light Vinaigrette, imported caviar, plump oysters, or tiny, sweet clams.

Another superb way to start your meal is with an enticing soup. The Billi-Bi, a lovely, creamy wonder, is prepared with fresh mussels, and it is exceptional. It is a distinctive dish and deserves four stars on its own merits.

Among the familiar favorites on the oversized menu at La Cote Basque are grilled sole, filet of beef, duck with peaches and a number of wonderful veal dishes that echo the culinary wonders of your favorite European restaurant. True to all fine kitchens, this noted chef at La Cote Basque is painstaking in the preparation of all the classic sauces that adorn his masterpieces. Try dumplings of pike or sole in lobster and champagne sauce. Then you will know the glories of a talented and experienced saucier!

A meal at La Cote Basque ends with a whiff of ecstasy from this remarkable kitchen. That is the frosting on the cake . . . the ethereal desserts. There are souffles and then there are souffles! Chocolate, orange, Grand Marnier. At many of the restaurants I visit, these are the favorites. Not so at La Cote Basque. From this amazing French kitchen come a never-ending supply of the most enticing Lemon Souffles known to man. Light and absolutely dreamy to bite into, these souffles are a fitting finale for a memorable meal.

Mme. Henriette Spalter, one of the owners, is greatly responsible for the continuance of this noted restaurant. She was an integral part of the original Pavillon during its heyday, and she will settle for nothing less than the best in quality dining. I admire her spunk. A million words have been written about her rules and regulations — including her insistence that women will not be admitted in pants. Ever. It all boils down to great simplicity as far as this restaurant writer is concerned . . . act like a lady, and you are apt to be treated like one.

Adding a special note of hospitality and welcome, Albert Spalter is a gracious host. He is Mme. Spalter's nephew and was of tremendous help in supplying us with recipes for this book. You are apt to see him greeting guests and talking with newcomers . . . or helping with a choice of wine . . . or seeing that countless details are handled with quiet efficiency.

As you linger over dessert, nibbling the luscious sweets and having coffee or brandy, you know that you have experienced the ultimate in American restaurants . . . the brainchild of a maestro. With all the remarkable specialties on the menu, with all the charm of decor and flowers, it seems certain that Henri Soule would be proud to have his name still beckoning people who love fine food to stop in for a fantastic visit and meal at La Cote Basque.

Filet of Sole en Goujons

from La Cote Basque

3 eggs
1 oz. milk
1 oz. oil
Salt and pepper
½ cup bread crumbs

¼ cup flour
2 pounds sole,
    cut into filets
Cooking oil to deep fry

Beat eggs with milk, oil, and seasoning. Cut the fillets diagonally across in pieces one half inch wide. Dip pieces of fish in flour, shaking well to remove excess. Dip in bread crumbs.

Heat enough oil to deep fry the fish. Fry until golden. Remove from oil and drain. Serve with mustard sauce.

Mustard sauce:

½ cup mayonnaise
½ cup sour cream
2 T. prepared mustard

1 T. prepared horseradish
2 tsp. dry mustard

Blend all ingredients. Serve with Filet of Sole.

Braised Striped Bass

from La Cote Basque

1 4-pound Bass
Salt and pepper
2 bay leaves, broken
¼ tsp. thyme
1½ cup dry white wine
1 cup fish stock

2 T. melted butter
½ cup fresh mushrooms,
    sliced
3 stalks celery, minced
2 T. parsley, minced
4 shallots, chopped fine

Clean the bass and season inside with salt and pe[...]per. Spread with thyme and bay leaves. Place the fisn in a small roasting pan that has been buttered. Top with celery, parsley, mushrooms and shallots.

Pour wine over the top and add fish stock. Sprinkle with melted butter. Bring to a boil and then cook in a 350 degree oven 30 to 40 minutes. Baste frequently.

Drain the fish. Place on serving dish and keep warm. Strain the liquid into a saucepan and boil down until half the volume, stirring well. Add 3 or 4 T. melted butter. Correct seasonings. Garnish and serve hot.

Serves 6.

Chicken Sauté Beausejour

from La Cote Basque

One 2½ lb. chicken	2 cloves garlic, minced
Salt and pepper	1 cup white wine
2 T. butter	¼ cup chicken stock
3 pinches thyme	2 T. parsley, chopped
2 broken bay leaves	

Cut chicken into serving pieces. Split the breast into two pieces and remove from the carcass. Season chicken with salt and pepper. Melt butter in a frying pan. Brown chicken well on both sides and cook over low heat for 20 minutes.

Sprinkle chicken with thyme, bay leaves and garlic. Add wine and chicken stock. Stir and cover. Cook slowly until liquids are reduced in volume one half and chicken is tender. Sprinkle with parsley.

French Apple Tart

from La Cote Basque

1 recipe for sweet
pastry crust (see
below)

3½ lbs. (about nine)
Golden delicious
apples

12 T. butter

1 one-inch stick, vanilla
bean

¼ cup confectioners'
sugar

½ cup marmalade

2 T. water

2 T. Grand Marnier

¼ cup slivered almonds,
toasted

Roll out the pastry dough on a very cold surface. Carefully place it in a 10-inch flan ring or pie plate and refrigerate.

Preheat oven to 400 degrees.

Peel apples; cut them in half and remove the cores. Pick out the ten best looking apple halves for the top of the tart. Cut the ends off these halves and set them aside.

Cut the rest of the apples into quarters and then into thin slices. Melt 8 tablespoons of butter in a large heavy skillet. Add the thinly sliced apples and the vanilla bean. Cook and stir the apples for about 30 minutes. When cooked they will be dry and browned. Now stir in the rest of the butter and add the browned apple slices to the pie plate.

Thinly slice the remaining apple halves and arrange them neatly in an overlapping pattern over the cooked apples. Using a sieve, sprinkle the tart with confectioners' sugar. Bake for one hour.

Meanwhile mix together the marmalade and water in a saucepan. Stir for several minutes until the mixture becomes thinner. Allow it to cool and stir in the Grand Marnier. Spread it over the cooked tart. Top with toasted almonds.

Serves 10 to 12.

Sweet Pastry Crust

from La Cote Basque

¼ lb. very cold butter, cut into small pieces
½ cup confectioners' sugar
2 egg yolks
1¼ cups flour
pinch of salt
½ to 1 tablespoon ice water

Place the butter, sugar and egg yolks in a mixing bowl and combine thoroughly with your hands or an electric beater. Put the flour and salt into a sifter and gradually add flour alternately with the water to the egg yolk mixture. Use only the amount of water needed to hold the mixture together. When it holds, form into a flat cake and wrap it in wax paper. Place in the refrigerator for a half hour. This will make a 9 to 10 inch crust.

El Parador

It is not often that one learns his trade from his mother-in-law. But that's how it was for Carlos Jacott who as the owner of the Mexican restaurant, El Parador, has gone on to become one of the most successful restaurateurs in the city of New York.

Carlos, a native of Chihuahua, Mexico first learned about restaurants waiting on tables while going to college in Iowa. But his knowledge of Mexican cooking comes from Mrs. Meano Garcia who besides being Carlos' mother-in-law owns El Charro . . . a restaurant serving excellent Mexican food in Greenwich Village.

With his teacher close by, Carlos opened El Parador in 1958. Today El Parador is not only a fine Mexican restaurant, it is also one of the liveliest eating places in all of the city. Nowhere in New York have I seen such crowds of enthusiastic diners, none of whom seem to be deterred by the long wait of an hour or more for a table.

Several years ago when El Parador moved from its small quarters on Second Avenue its faithful patrons thought they had it made. No more dinners at midnight or tacos eaten hurriedly at the bar. But this never happened. Fanciers of Mexican cooking and El Parador keep growing. Even with dining rooms on two levels, El Parador can still boast the longest and pleasantest wait for a table in town. Located on East 34th Street (between First and Second Avenues), El Parador serves dinner only every evening except Sunday. No reservations are accepted.

Most restaurant guides praise El Parador for having the best Mexican food in town. But it is not only the good food that makes El Parador a great place to go to. It's also the atmosphere created by the hardworking Carlos, a handsome gentleman who is easily recognized in his black tie. Carlos is one of the most charming hosts in the city and everyone feels welcome.

27

When you enter this restaurant you will find yourself in a seductively lit bar room decorated with attractive Mexican furnishings. The large wooden bar is never found empty. Finding a place to stand among the models, actors, executives and professional people who frequent El Parador often takes a bit of friendly maneuvering. But that's all part of the fun of spending an evening here. Once you have one of the bartenders' spectacular Margaritas in hand time passes quickly and you'll find you don't mind waiting.

Carlos, operating with the efficiency of a computer and the charm of a diplomat helps direct you to seats at the bar that are soon to be vacated by guests ready to move into the dining area. At the bar you can dip some fried tortilla chips into the tasty chili sauce and loosen up your taste buds for the spicy food ahead. No names are taken when you arrive, but miraculously everyone gets seated just in the order of their arrival.

A recent dinner began with Ceviche . . . raw fish fillets marinated in lime juice and spices. We are including the recipe for this tasty appetizer in our cookbook. It's so simple to prepare and what's more there's not even any cooking involved in preparing this dish. Just stop by your local fish store and buy some fresh snapper, flounder or scallops. Marinate the fish overnight in the lime juice. The fish is "cooked" by the fresh lime juice. Both you and your guests will be surprised by the results.

Another excellent beginner is nachos, which are tortilla chips topped with refried beans and cheese that are melted in the broiler. If you're still drinking Margaritas they are an excellent accompaniment. Sometimes we order Nachos at the bar. Many diners here also like to start their meal with Guacamole, the well known mashed avocado mixed with garlic, tomatoes and spices and served with Tortilla chips.

Mexican combination plates of tacos, enchiladas, tamales and tostados are the popular main dishes. There are ten combinations to choose from and all are worth a try. If you are discovering Mexican food for the first time and don't know your tacos from your nachos, the back of the menu explains all. The menu gently points out that it is proper to eat the tacos and tostados with your hands.

In addition to the combination platters, there are many other spicy entrees to tempt you. The chicken mole, flavored with a touch of chocolate and spices is a favorite. If you order this chicken you will probably think the waiter made a mistake when you see two similar sized plates piled in front of you. When the first is filled with the bones it will be taken away . . . and you continue eating from a clean plate.

The five shrimp dishes listed on the menu are each made with a totally different sauce. They include a special creole, a chile and a green sauce. The shrimp are served piping hot in attractive enameled pots by one of Carlos' polite and efficient waiters. Side orders are special too. Most people enjoy the refried beans with melted cheese served with a basket of soft warm tortillas.

All the main dishes come with a salad, rice, beans and tortilla chips. Everything is served a la carte with main dishes priced from $5.25 to $6.50, moderate for New York but higher than the other Mexican restaurants in town. With your dinner we recommend an ice cold glass of one of the fine Mexican beers. Sangria and Spanish wines are also available. For dessert flan (carmel custard) and Natilla (Spanish cream) are good choices.

Most dishes are on the spicy-hot side but even those who prefer milder food can find something to please them. A dinner of tasty tacos, enchiladas and chiles

29

from our neighbor to the South is always a welcome change. New York is fortunate to have dedicated and knowledgeable restaurateurs such as Carlos to offer so many Mexican specialties right at home. When we asked Carlos for recipes for our cookbook he felt honored and we are pleased to include some of his finest dishes.

Margarita

from El Parador

2 oz. tequila
1 oz. Triple Sec or
  cointreau

1 oz. lemon juice
salt

Dip a cocktail glass in ice water. Pour salt on a plate and dip the rim of the glass into the salt so that it becomes lightly coated with the salt.

Put the tequila, Triple Sec and lemon juice into a cocktail shaker. Shake well and strain into the glass.

Serves one.

Chicken Mexican Style

from El Parador

2 chickens (about 4
lbs. each) cut into
serving pieces
¼ cup peanut oil
2 cups onions, finely
chopped
¼ cup jalapenos or
chile serranos,
chopped
2 T. garlic, chopped
¼ cup mushrooms,
finely chopped

1 cup green pepper,
finely chopped
1 T. flour
6 bay leaves
1 tsp. M.S.G.
1 tsp. oregano
2 cans tomato paste,
6 oz. size
6 cups beef broth
3 cups cold water
salt and pepper to taste

Heat oil in a large pan. Add onions, jalapenos, garlic, mushrooms and green pepper. Cook, stirring frequently until onions are golden brown.

While stirring add flour, water, oregano, bay leaves, M.S.G., tomato paste and broth.

Drop chicken into the sauce and continue cooking, stirring occasionally for about 2 hours. Season to taste with salt and pepper.

Serves 8.

Note: canned Jalapenos or chiles serranos are very hot, so add a small amount and taste. They can be purchased at Casa Moneo, 210, West 14th Street, New York City.

Ceviche

from El Parador

2 cups fish fillets
  (flounder, red
  snapper or scallops)
½ cup onions, chopped
2 large chile jalapenos
  or 4 small chile ser-
  ranos, finely chopped
½ cup fresh lime juice

½ cup olive oil
1 ripe tomato, chopped
2 cloves garlic, minced
½ tsp. thyme
1 T. parsley, chopped
½ cup sweet red pepper,
  finely chopped
salt and pepper to taste

Cut the fish into ½ inch cubes. Combine all the ingredients and let stand in the refrigerator overnight. Be sure to use a glass container. The fish will be cooked by the fresh lime juice.

Serves 8.

Note: The fish used should be as fresh as possible. Peppers can be purchased at Casa Moneo, 210 West 14th Street, N. Y. C.

Guacamole

from El Parador

1 ripe avocado (the size of a small grapefruit)

3 T. onion, finely chopped

2 cloves garlic, finely chopped

1 chile serrano, chopped (you can substitute ¼ tsp. tabasco sauce)

salt and pepper to taste

Peel and chop the avocado; then mash it with a fork or potato masher. Now mix all the ingredients together.

The following ingredients may also be added: 1 small ripe tomato, peeled and chopped; 1 to 2 tablespoons fresh lemon or lime juice; 1 to 2 strips of crisp fried bacon, chopped; 1 to 2 tablespoons coriander leaves, chopped.

Serves 2-3.

Flower Drum

Flower Drum is a jewel of a Chinese restaurant. Dishes here are dazzling to look at as well as to eat; service is like a fine French restaurant and there's even a touch of The Four Seasons with a menu that changes every three months to offer seasonal specialties.

In this city which offers an endless variety of Chinese restaurants this is the one place that you'll find yourself going back to after you've traveled the Szechuan, Hunan, Peking, Shanghai and Cantonese circuit. For all these regional cuisines are offered right at Flower Drum.

Tastes here run the gamut from bland to tingling hot. It is evident that owner Peter Lee knows and cares about Chinese cuisine. He takes time to help you compose a meal. Mr. Lee will work out a very tasty arrangement of whatever you select. He insures your dining pleasure by seeing that only one or two dishes are served at a time so that you can dine more leisurely and enjoy each marvelous taste. As the creations arrive they are announced and described by a friendly waiter.

The decor is the only unspectacular feature of this midtown Chinese restaurant. It has a usual display of lanterns, chimes and fans. On the plus side the restaurant is divided into sections and tables are far enough apart for comfortable dining. Flower Drum is open every day for lunch and dinner. Hours during the week are from 11:30 a.m. until 3 p.m. and from 5 to 11 p.m. On Saturdays the restaurant stays open from noon until midnight and on Sunday from 1 to 11 p.m. Dinner here should run about $8 per person.

Flower Drum is located on Second Avenue just a block from the United Nations and is a favorite dining spot of many delegates. This is quite understandable since Mr. Lee worked as a calligrapher for the United

Nations before coming to Flower Drum in 1963. You can always tell by the crowds at lunch when the General Assembly is in session. When the Peking delegations to the United Nations first arrived in New York in 1972 it was Flower Drum that prepared the sumptuous banquet for its first official welcome party, and what a welcome it was. The 12 course gourmet banquet was cooked in the Flower Drum kitchen and whisked around the corner to the U.N. You can enjoy this very same banquet any night at the restaurant by requesting it in advance. The cost is about $10 per person.

The adventurous menu is four pages long. Mr. Lee respects the seasonal availability of many foods. A special section of the menu is devoted to delicacies of each season. He feels that "certain foods reach their high peak of natural flavor at special seasons." The menu also incorporates the concept that "foods offering warmth and energy are favored during the winter months and those that are light and cool are best enjoyed in summer."

Our first trip to Flower Drum was at the beginning of the summer. It was a hot night and we began our dinner with some Szechuan spicy salad. As one of the main dishes Mr. Lee recommended Squab in Jade Nest . . . minced squab sauteed with fresh Chinese vegetables in an oyster sauce; wrapped in a lettuce leaf and eaten like a taco. A good recommendation it was. We decided to pass up the chicken made with fresh lichees that evening in favor of some shredded spicy beef served on a crisp scallion pancake. Danny Kaye recently described it as elegant Chinese Pizza. Next we enjoyed a marvelous creation of fresh filet of sole and mushrooms gently steeped in a tasty rice wine sauce.

Fresh lichees are available for only six weeks a year beginning in late spring. Mr. Lee likes to recount an

36

old Chinese story about an army officer who rode 4,000 miles to South Canton to purchase fresh lichees for the emperor's wife. Supposedly the people were so enraged by this outrageous use of military personnel for satisfying the whims of nobility that a war broke out. For six weeks in New York City when served over ice at the Flower Drum lichees are a perfect summer dessert.

In the fall when we visited Flower Drum we found out that Mr. Lee had just spent a good part of the day perfecting a spicy new fresh crab dish. Hearing about our cookbook Mr. Lee invited us into the kitchen to see how it was made. Fresh blue crabs in the shell were cooked quickly in very hot oil and then mixed with black bean paste, scallions and other seasonings. It was one of the most incredible Chinese dishes we had ever eaten. We were happy that Mr. Lee saved his new crab dish for last. There's really not much you could serve after this imaginative creation. The dish will appear on the Flower Drum menu in the fall. In the meanwhile it is not difficult to prepare at home.

When winter comes the restaurant features heavier dishes such as the Fire Pot which originated in Northern China. Each diner cooks his own chicken, fish or beef and vegetables in a bubbling soup (fondue style) and then dips the cooked food into a variety of exotic sauces. Afterwards you may drink the soup.

Another page of the menu is devoted to regional dishes from Szechuan, Hunan, Canton, Peking and Shanghai. Mr. Lee explained that the topography and climate of China have resulted in the wide variety of cuisines. Szechuan's humid mountain valleys are rich in spices . . . while the coastal village of Canton abounds in seafood.

Flower Drum does some wonderful things with seafood. Our favorites in this category are the Gang

Jen Shrimp (They're quickly sauteed and combined with oyster sauce and sesame oil; then topped with shredded scallions.) and the Shrimp Supreme Flower Drum. Here shrimp are coated with a spicy sauce that contains fresh chopped water chestnuts. We often enjoy these dishes together as an appetizer.

Before you leave your waiter will arrive at your table with a complimentary brass tea pot of plum wine, "a drink of happiness", and some incredible fresh roasted candied walnuts, another treat that Mr. Lee shared the recipe for with us. It is a delightful way to end your feast here and even if you are not a dignitary from Peking or a noted celebrity you go home feeling like one.

Crab Meat Su Szu Wei

from Flower Drum

¼ lb. crab meat cut
    into large pieces
¼ cup pea pods
¼ cup fresh water
    chestnuts, sliced
½ cup baby corn

1/3 tsp. salt
1 T. cornstarch
1 tsp. rice wine
½ tsp. sugar
5 T. consomme

Heat consomme in a wok or heavy skillet. Add crab meat and vegetables to the pan. Cook for 2 to 3 minutes over a medium flame. When cooked add cornstarch, rice wine, salt and sugar. Mix together and cook for a minute or two. Serve hot.

Serves 2.

Shrimp Supreme

from Flower Drum

1 lb. medium sized shrimp	dash of salt
	2 T. ketchup
3 fresh water chestnuts peeled and finely chopped	1 tsp. sesame oil
	1 T. consomme
	1½ cups vegetable oil
2 egg whites	3 scallions, finely chopped
1 cup, 1 T. cornstarch	

Clean shrimps. Slice in half lengthwise.

Beat egg whites until slightly frothy. Then add 1 tablespoon cornstarch and a dash of salt. Place shrimps in the mixture, making sure they are coated thoroughly.

Place the cup of cornstarch in a separate bowl and douse each shrimp with the cornstarch. Then put shrimp on a separate plate and set aside.

In a separate bowl combine the ketchup, water chestnuts, sesame oil, consomme and mix well. Set aside.

Heat oil in a wok or heavy skillet. Add shrimps, stirring gently until they start turning brown. Remove from pan and place on paper towels to drain.

In another skillet heat one tablespoon of the oil. Spread around sides. Add sauce mixture and stir. Then add shrimps. Cook for about ten seconds. Just before removing shrimps from pan sprinkle the scallions over shrimp and serve. Shrimps should be dry and crispy.

Serves 2 to 4.

Tsao Liu Yu Pien

(fish filets in wine sauce)

from Flower Drum

½ lb. fish fillets
1 egg white
1½ T. cornstarch
1 cup, 1 T. corn oil
1/3 tsp. salt
2 cloves garlic, chopped
4 T. consomme

4 T. rice wine
3 T. sugar
¼ cup tree fungus (dry),
　soaked
1 T. cornstarch mixed
　with 1 T. water

Combine egg white, cornstarch, 1 tablespoon oil and salt. Mix with fish fillets.

Heat remaining oil in a heavy skillet or wok. When oil is hot add fish. Cook and stir for about 1½ minutes. Then remove fish and all but about 1 tablespoon of oil from the skillet.

Reheat oil in skillet and add the garlic, rice wine, sugar, fungus and cornstarch mixed with water. Stir ingredients together and cook for about a minute. Then add fish. Heat thoroughly and serve.

Serves 2.

Gang Jen Shrimp

from Flower Drum

½ lb. medium sized
　shrimp
½ cup flour
1 T. salad oil

1 tsp. sugar
2 T. oyster sauce
½ tsp. sesame oil
1 scallion

Remove veins and clean shrimp. Pour flour over shrimp. Moisten with 2 tablespoons water.

Cut scallion into fine slices. set aside.

Heat the oil in a heavy skillet (or wok) and add shrimp. Pan fry shrimp under a medium heat until brown on both sides. Then add the sugar, oyster sauce and sesame oil to the pan and cook over a high flame for a minute or two. Remove shrimp from pan. Top with shredded scallions and serve.

Serves 2 to 3.

Roasted Walnuts

from Flower Drum

1 lb. shelled walnuts	3 cups peanut oil
¼ lb. sugar	water

Put walnuts in a wok or skillet and cover with water. The water should be one inch above walnuts. Bring to a boil and stir for about 10 minutes. Drain.

Now add water to just cover walnuts. Bring to a boil and add sugar, stirring constantly to make sure sugar dissolves. Continue stirring until water has evaporated (about 15 minutes).

Immediately transfer nuts to another skillet and add oil until it is one inch over walnuts. Fry over a high heat for about 5 to 7 minutes. As walnuts brown, remove and drain. Spread to avoid sticking. Cool and serve.

Serves 6.

Crabs in the Shell

from Flower Drum

6 fresh crabs	2 scallions, cut into
1 cup corn oil	fine strips
2 T. sherry or rice wine	1 T. black bean paste
2 T. consomme	1 sweet red pepper,
2 T. light colored	minced
soy sauce	2 cloves garlic, sliced
2 T. sugar	4 slices ginger root
1 T. corn oil	1 T. cornstarch

Mix together the sherry, consomme, soy sauce and sugar. Set aside.

Tear each crab apart. Cut off shell covering stomache. Split bottom in half. Cut off all inedible portions. Hit claws to crack shell.

Heat the cup of oil in a wok or heavy skillet. When the oil is very hot add the crabs and cook and stir over a high flame for several minutes. Then remove crabs and pour oil from the skillet. Now add scallions, bean paste, red pepper, ginger and garlic to the same pan and cook for about 2 minutes. Add mixture of sherry, consomme, soy sauce and sugar to the pan and combine all ingredients.

Then put crabs back into the skillet. Cover and cook for 3 to 5 minutes so that meat inside the shell is cooked. Then add 1 tablespoon of oil (to make crabs shiny) and 1 tablespoon of cornstarch. Stir well and serve immediately.

Serves 3 to 4.

Squab in Jade Nest

from Flower Drum

1 squab	1 tsp. salt
4 fresh water chestnuts, minced	2 T. sugar
½ cup peas	2 tsp. oyster sauce
1/3 cup dried mushrooms, minced	1½ tsp. sesame oil
	1½ tsp. soy sauce
1 cup corn oil for frying	4 large iceberg lettuce leaves

Remove squab meat from bones. Discard skin and mince squab into small pieces. Set aside.

Mix together the water chestnuts, dried mushrooms and peas.

Heat oil in a wok or heavy skillet. When hot add the squab. Cook and stir for several minutes. Remove squab and oil from the pan, leaving about 1 tablespoon of the oil in the pan. Drain squab.

Heat remaining oil and add the water chestnuts, dried mushrooms and peas. Stir fry for one minute. Then add the salt, sugar, oyster sauce, sesame oil and soy sauce. Blend these ingredients with the vegetables. Add squab and mix it with all the other ingredients.

Arrange lettuce leaves on a platter and spoon mixture on leaves. Wrap each leaf like a taco and serve.

Serves 2 to 4.

Note: A good oyster sauce is necessary for success here. The brand used at the Flower Drum is Fook Cheong Hing.

Four Seasons

There is an urgent rapidity about the change of seasons in New York. Brief teasings of springtime rush into extended heat waves . . . autumn barely touches the horizon and disappears into gusts of wintry cold. It is not too often that we think of seasonal changes. That is, of course, until we visit that exciting restaurant that sets its moods and yours on the enchanting changes and colors of winter, spring, summer, and autumn — The Four Seasons.

This ingenious and carefully planned change from one season to another is masterfully executed with flowering plants, different menus for each season, a change in table linen, and even a new "costume" for the skillful waiters. The entire concept is magnificent, and dining in this showplace restaurant is a thrilling experience. Not only are you dazzled by the marble fountain that is centered in the room, but by the handsome art and fabulous view of the city.

Much can be said about elegant surroundings. To me, it is the wonders of nature that make this restaurant such a marvel. The unique way that The Four Seasons has utilized the most perfect fruits and vegetables is a delight in esthetics as well as taste.

James Beard has been called "a founding father of The Four Seasons and a principal contributor to the development of its seasonal food concept." My own introduction, initially, was to the restaurant's marvelous cookbook, which I used long before I had the experience of dining here. It is a "one of its kind" among the 7,000 cookbooks that have flooded the American book market. The recipes are divided into four sections, each devoted to one of the seasons.

Located in the Seagram Building at 99 East 52nd Street, the Four Seasons restaurant was the dream of Joseph Baum. Since his dream was first conceived, many years of seasons have come and gone, and with

45

each menu there have been changes and improvements to expand a reputation that has made this an "institution" to people who know and appreciate good food.

First courses of interest are smoked salmon souffle in a flaky pastry crust, wonderful shrimp filled with Italian fruits, (the recipe is included), fried oysters in horseradish sauce, stuffed mussels, or crab-meat crepes. You may also begin a meal with unusual soups, sampling such variations as apricot with sour cream or avocado soup with avocado sherbet.

An enormous offering of superb entrees is available. One long-time favorite is the entrecote for two, a juicy steak cut like a huge lamb chop. Steaks may be flavored with such exotic seasonings and sauces that their superb quality is matched by the inventive preparation. Seafood is prepared in numerous ways and baby lamb is garnished and roasted to perfection.

Guests are invited to chose their favorite vegetables from baskets, and the vegetables are rushed to the kitchen and prepared to order. Such an array of flavorful vegetables . . . baby corn and tiny eggplant, squash, carrots, and tomatoes. Asparagus is prepared in many delicious ways . . . a delicate sauce maltaise flavored with orange may enhance this one day or a scrumptious hazelnut butter another.

Guests who frequent this special restaurant may enjoy a number of entrees rarely found elsewhere. Duckling is prepared with peaches and cassis; venison is soaked in marinade and peppered to an exquisite flavor; and pheasant is stuffed with a well-seasoned sausage dressing.

Perhaps my love for desserts has been the strongest bond with The Four Seasons. There is no other restaurant in the country that surpasses their memorable dessert cart. You may taste such ecstacy as white chocolate ice cream, The Four Seasons Fancy Cake, French rice pudding, hazelnut cake with creamy filling, meringues, and souffles of every description. The piece de resistance is their famous Chocolate Velvet Four Seasons. I laugh when I pick up my Four Seasons cookbook, for on page 76 where this recipe can be found, there are drippings of a hundred chocolate-covered spoons, used in all these years of preparing that spectacular dessert. It is sensational, and if you prepare it at home, you can use very thinly sliced, fresh pound cake instead of the sponge cake, and achieve a delicious result.

Behind every great restaurant there is an ambitious man . . . in the case of The Four Seasons, there are many men who have been responsible for the restaurants development. Paul Kovi, the manager, has been our link with the wonders of each season, and we are grateful to him for his courtesy and for the marvelous recipes which we hope our readers will try with enthusiasm.

Nature has created a wonderful assortment of wonders in the cycle of each year. Our pleasures of a lifetime are often associated with a particular time of the calendar. It is a mystery that has inspired poets and artists since the beginning of time. And this wonderful and innovative appreciation of every month of the year is most loved by gourmands from around the world . . . at The Four Seasons!

Crisped Shrimp with Mustard Fruit

from The Four Seasons

24 large shrimp
3 cups court bouillon
1 cup cremonese Mustard
   Fruit, with liquid
4 cups flour
2 tbsp. oil
1 tsp. baking powder
3 cups water

2 egg yolks
Salt to taste
Flour for Dipping
2 cups sauce Bechamel
2 tbsp. dry mustard
6 tbsp. mustard fruit,
   in chunks

Poach shrimp in court-bouillon until they turn pink or for about 4 minutes. Drain. Shell and de-vein. Mince the cup of mustard fruit in their liquid. Slit shrimp halfway through and stuff with the minced fruit. Pat firmly so that the stuffing remains in the shrimp.

Make a thick batter by mixing the flour, oil, baking powder, water, egg yolks, and salt. Roll shrimp in the flour, then dip into the batter. Deep fry in 400-degree oil until brown. (4 to 6 minutes) Drain.

Mix Bechamel with mustard and the mustard fruit. Heat. Serve in a separate dish as sauce for the shrimp.

Serves 6 appetizers or 4 entrees

Sauce Bechamel

from The Four Seasons

½ stick butter   1 carrot sliced

½ cup flour   ½ onion, stuck with

1 quart of milk, heated 4 cloves

Bouquet Garni (Parsley, Bay Leaf, and Celery)

Melt the butter. Stir in the flour, a little at a time, until smooth. Cook over a low heat a few minutes. Then add the milk gradually. Stir until thickened. Add the carrot, onion and bouquet garni. Simmer 10 minutes and strain.

Makes about 4 cups

Artichoke Bottoms Stuffed with Spinach

from The Four Seasons

1 lb. fresh spinach 12 cooked artichoke

4 Tbsp. butter   bottoms

Salt to taste   1½ c. thick Bechamel

Dash of nutmeg   sauce

Dash of freshly   6 Tbsp. grated

 ground pepper   parmesan cheese

Blanch spinach 3 minutes in boiling water, drain well, and mince fine. Saute in butter and add seasonings. Heap mixture on artichoke bottoms. Top each with 2 Tbsp. Bechamel. Sprinkle with grated cheese. Run under broiler to brown. Serves 6.

Roquefort Steak

from The Four Seasons

6 12-oz. shell steaks, trimmed of all fat	¼ lb. butter
Salt and pepper	¼ lb. Roquefort cheese, crumbled
¼ c. oil	

Very lightly salt and pepper steaks. Put oil and 2 Tbsp. butter in a skillet and saute' steaks over fairly high heat — 5 minutes each side for rare, 7 minutes for medium, and 10 for well done. Remove steaks to serving platter and keep warm. Pour fat from pan and replace pan over heat. Melt remaining butter in pan. Stir Roquefort thoroughly into butter, pour over steaks, and serve. Serves 6.

Potatoes Parisienne

from The Four Seasons

3 pounds large potatoes	¼ cup oil
¼ cup butter	Salt and pepper to taste

Peel and wash the potatoes. Cut into little balls with the large end of a ball cutter. Blanch for 5 minutes in boiling water. Drain the potatoes and cool under cold running water. Dry on paper towels.

Heat the oil and butter in a heavy skillet until very hot. Add the potatoes and sprinkle them with salt and pepper. Cook slowly, shaking the skillet from time to time until the potatoes are brown. Serves 6

Peaches Flamed in Bourbon

from The Four Seasons

6 peaches, peeled and halved	¾ c. sugar
	½ c. peach nectar
1 c. bourbon	Crushed macaroons
¼ c. butter	

Soak peaches in bourbon 24 hours. Drain and reserve bourbon. Melt butter in a large skillet, add sugar and cook until caramelized. Add peaches, flat side down. Cook until slightly browned, turn and repeat. Heat ¼ c. of the bourbon and pour over peaches. Ignite. Shake pan until flames die. Pour in peach nectar; heat a few moments. Place flat side up on serving dish. Sprinkle with crushed macaroons and serve. Serves 6.

Sugar-Glazed Strawberries

from The Four Seasons

2 c. sugar

2/3 c. water

Perfect strawberries,
not hulled

Heat sugar and water in saucepan, stirring constantly, until syrup reaches "crack" stage (270 degrees on a candy thermometer). Place saucepan in pan of hot water. Holding strawberries by stems, dip into syrup. Cover completely except for stems. Place on oiled surface to harden.

Raspberry Sherbet

from The Four Seasons

3 pints raspberries (or enough to make 1 pint pureé)

1½ pints simple syrup (2 c. water and 1 c. sugar, boiled 5 minutes, cooled)

Juice of 2 whole lemons (or to taste)

Puree fruit in blender, sieve or food mill. Beat with syrup and lemon juice. Taste and adjust tartness if necessary. Freeze a test sample. If sample is icy, add a little syrup; if too soft, add a little water. Pour into the container of an electric ice-cream freezer and let it turn 20 minutes. Makes 1 quart.

Chocolate Velvet Four Seasons

from The Four Seasons

1 11"x16" sponge cake
3 egg yolks
1 Tbsp. instant coffee
¼ c. kirsch
¼ c. rum
¼ c. creme de cacao
1/3 c. canned praline paste, firmly packed

6 Tbsp. melted butter, hot
1½ lbs. melted semi-sweet chocolate, hot
3 egg whites
Pinch of salt
¼ c. confectioners' sugar
2 c. heavy cream, whipped, unsweetened

Line a round 1-quart mold with sponge cake by cutting out a round to fit bottom of mold and strips to cover sides. Reserve any remaining cake. Mix yolks, coffee, kirsch, rum, creme de cacao and praline paste. Beat until smooth. Add hot melted butter, then hot melted chocolate. Add salt to egg whites and beat until they form soft peaks. Add sugar, a tbsp. at a time, beating well after each addition. Beat until very stiff, about 5 minutes. Fold whipped cream and egg whites into original mixture. Pour into mold. Refrigerate 2 hours, or until firm. Cover top with remaining cake. Loosen sides of mold with sharp knife. Invert on a plate. Frost all over with semi-sweet icing and chill.

Semi-sweet chocolate icing:

5 squares semi-sweet chocolate

¼ c. boiling water

Melt chocolate and mix with water, blending well.

Granados

Small, unpretentious and located just off Washington Square in Greenwich Village, Granados has been a favorite Spanish kitchen of native New Yorkers for over 25 years. Granados seems to effortlessly maintain the ambiance of an old Village restaurant. Waiters never let you feel rushed and it is not uncommon for the proprietor, Lorenzo, to sit with you and talk for hours after dessert and coffee has been served.

A little well deserved bravado on the menu tells about the heritage of the restaurant. "Lorenzo de Granados, the father of Spanish cuisine in New York is happy to share the scientific culinary knowledge with you that it has taken 500 years of tradition to acquire." He has brought New York his family's best dishes. We are delighted that he is willing to share so many of his great classic recipes with us.

Lorenzo's expertise in Spanish cooking started during his boyhood days in Northwestern Spain where his family owned a restaurant for more than four centuries. As a young boy he spent many hours in his family's kitchen. Inspired by his uncle, Enrico Granados, a famous Spanish composer, he studied music in Europe. He then came to the United States to pursue a career as a concert pianist. When an accident resulted in an injured hand, he was unable to play the piano and naturally turned to his second love . . . the kitchen.

Granados opened in 1947. It is as close as you can get to typical Spanish cuisine without boarding a plane. The decor is typical too . . . original Goya engravings hanging on white stucco walls, beamed ceilings and blue and white Spanish tile table tops in a small 60 seat dining room.

Lorenzo is a charming man now in his seventies who likes to recount how many of the waiters and chefs he has trained have left and opened up Spanish restaurants all over the city. Today Lorenzo is still very devoted to his work and keeps a watchful eye over his kitchen as well as his customers.

If Lorenzo is unable to meet you at the door, he's probably downstairs in the kitchen tending the meat and fowl which are hung to dry in a special brick oven. He will certainly arrive in time to help you select your dinner. Use the menu to practice your Spanish, but let Lorenzo be your guide.

Lorenzo claims there are too many people going to Spanish restaurants who have never gotten past eating paella. He feels that this is unfortunate. His paella is a beautiful authentic dish of saffron rice, seafood, meat and chicken brought to the table in a large paella pan. It will please you, but not Lorenzo, since there are so many other great spanish dishes to be discovered. When he can, Lorenzo encourages ordering family style so everyone can get to taste a few dishes.

An evening at Granados often starts with a large pitcher of brandy spiked Sangria. Further into the meal the regulars usually switch to Rioja (Spanish wine). Lorenzo's love of music is evident. There is always Spanish music in the background and often a flamenco guitarist.

Appetizers are not listed on the menu. A pleasant way to start your dinner is with an order of shrimp in wine sauce, one of the specialties we've included in this book. Tasty bite sized marinated spare ribs make another excellent beginning. A good Gazpacho is also available.

For an unusual entree try the Lemon Sole Contabric in Master Sauce. It's a crisp broiled filet of sole topped with a special sauce with a hint of lemon. Other specialties we've enjoyed here numerous times are veal with an almond sauce and quail in fruit sauce. Granados also prepares a gourmet duck that is unlike anything in New York. Cut into small pieces and served with a fruit based sauce it is always a treat. All entrees come with rice or thinly sliced home made potato chips and a salad with a tangy tomato dressing that is so popular Lorenzo bottles it for his patrons to take home.

Many traditional Spanish dinners end with Natilla (vanilla pudding) or Flan (a carmel custard). Granados does them both well. Spanish Manchego cheese and expresso are also available. Dinner for two with wine will cost about $25. Try lunch when the menu is the same but entrees are half price.

On Sunday special regional dishes are served. Popular during the winter is Cucido, a stew containing beef, veal, sausage, smoked pork, cabbage and potatoes all blended together. Lorenzo is a proud chef and will roast a baby lamb or cook any other Spanish dish you desire. Just call him a day or two in advance. He is also happy to help you out if you want to have a Spanish party or would like to enjoy some of these dishes at home with friends. Just drop off some pots. The duck and spare ribs travel especially well.

When you stop here in Greenwich Village, you will be dining with local "Villagers" who have been coming back for many years. Many come on the way to or from an off Broadway show and still others travel to the Village just to eat at Granados. If you never have the opportunity of visiting the sun streaked cafes along the Southeastern Mediterranean coast of Spain, yet long for the magical touch of Valencia . . . your dreams are right around the corner. For mingled in that international potpourri of tiny restaurants and coffee houses in Greenwich Village, you will discover one of the most lovable Spanish restaurants in America. This is, of course, Granados!

Mariscada

from Granados

6 lobster tails,
    4 oz. each
½ cup Spanish olive oil
2 or 3 cloves garlic
    halved
½ tsp. powdered ginger
1 lb. clams in shell
1 lb. large shrimp
    shelled
½ lb. scallops

4 to six scallions
½ cup Italian parsley,
    minced
2 T. flour
1 T. monsodium
    glutamate
2 eggs
1 cup milk or light cream
1 cup dry white wine
½ tsp. salt
dash pepper

Split lobster tails down the back vertically. Hold under hot running water for a few moments and pull flesh partially away from the shell. Heat olive oil in a heavy skillet. Add garlic and ginger. When garlic is brown remove it and set aside. Add all the shellfish to the oil. Cover and cook from 7 to 10 minutes. (When ready the clam shells open). While cooking chop the browned garlic with the scallions and mix with the parsley. Then blend together the flour, monosodium glutamate, eggs, milk and wine. Add salt and pepper and mix until smooth. When the shellfish are pink quickly stir the sauce into the oil in the pan. The eggs will look slightly curdled. Serve at once with hot, steamed white rice.

Serves 6 to 8.

Gazpacho Andaluz

from Granados

1 cup soft white
   bread crumbs
2 T. wine vinegar
3 large garlic cloves
1 tsp. salt
4 T. olive oil
1 large can peeled
   tomatoes (16 oz.) or
   six large, ripe
   tomatoes

water (about 2 cups)
   or beef stock
vinegar and salt to
   taste (optional)
1 large cucumber,
   peeled and diced
2 large green peppers,
   diced

Soak bread crumbs in the vinegar and crush with garlic cloves. Combine this with salt and olive oil in a mortar to make a paste. Then press tomatoes through a sieve to remove seeds. If fresh tomatoes are used, peel them and remove seeds, combine tomatoes in a blender with ingredients from the mortar and mix until smooth. Add water and chill thoroughly. More cold water, vinegar or salt may be added before serving. Garnish with cucumber and green peppers. In the summer, Gazpacho is often served, without the garnish as a drink.

Serves 4.

Note: During the summer Lorenzo likes to add some crushed seedless grapes or small cubes of melon.

Paella a la Valenciana

from Granados

2½ lbs. chicken, cut into serving pieces
¾ cup Spanish olive oil
2 cloves garlic
2 T. fresh parsley, minced
1 medium onion, minced
1 pimento, drained and chopped
½ tsp. saffron
¼ tsp. coriander, crushed

2 tsp. salt
1 qt. chicken stock
2 cups long grain rice
1 lb. large shrimp, peeled
4 small lobster tails (about 7 oz. each)
1 qt. mussels or clams, well scrubbed
1 cup peas
3 T. Spanish olive oil
2 T. Spanish sherry

Remove undershell of the lobster tails. Hold frozen tails under hot water a few moments. Then pull flesh partially away from hard upper shell. Cut each tail in half cutting right through the hard shell. Set aside.

Heat the ¾ cup olive oil in a large heavy skillet or casserole and saute chicken with the garlic and half of the onion. When garlic is browned remove from pan and set aside. Now add remaining onion, parsley and pimento to the pan. If necessary add more olive oil. Cook until the chicken is browned.

Crush saffron with the browned garlic and salt; stir in a tablespoon of warm water to dissolve and add mixture to the pan. Now add the rice and stir to glaze with olive oil. Slowly add the chicken stock and bring to a boil. Then lower flame and cook for ten minutes, shaking the pan occasionally to prevent the rice from sticking. Place lobster, shrimp, mussels or clams and peas on top of the rice. Simmer, uncovered for ten minutes, until most of the liquid is absorbed and the mussel shells are open. Sprinkle the remaining olive oil and sherry over the top of the mixture. Cover and steam over a very low heat for about 5 minutes. Serve from the casserole or pan.

Serves 8.

Natilla

from Granados

1 qt. milk	1 cup sugar
grated rind of 1 lemon	6 tsp. cornstarch
dash salt	1 cup cocktail sherry
1 cinnamon stick	6 T. cream sherry
4 eggs	

Mix the milk, lemon rind, salt and cinnamon stick together in a saucepan and bring to a boil. Then beat together the eggs, sugar and cornstarch. Add cocktail sherry. Strain the milk and pour into the beaten mixture; stir slowly until a paste is formed. Cook over a very low heat for 3 minutes. Pour into individual serving dishes and allow to cool. To serve sprinkle with cinnamon and use 1 Tablespoon of cream sherry over each portion.

Serves 6.

La Grenouille

If restaurateurs could be likened to environmentalists, there is one man who has beautified the world of New York Haute Cuisine to such an extent that his magnificent "lily pad" is the most fragrant and beautiful place to dine in the country. This gentleman is Charles Masson, who tends the most glamorous frog pond in the world!

In the midst of busy Manhattan, a cool, uninterrupted view of green, mirrored and wrapped around a garden of incredible fresh flowers, this outstanding restaurant is a breath of springtime four seasons of the year. Close to $40,000 yearly go into the dazzling arrangements of shaded roses, fresh daisies, and anemones that brighten the tables and stand around in massive, splendid arrangements of color throughout the dining room. To this luscious garden scene come the most beautiful people of society . . . royalty, theatrical talents, stockbrokers, literary giants, and the fashionable "400".

The beauty of the setting is matched by the exquisite French cuisine. Well known Charles Masson is the distinguished owner of this euphoria in New York. It is more than an eating place . . . it is a symbol of exalted plateau in the world of crumbling restaurant empires. A gracious host, charming and artistic, Mr. Masson blends Parisian glamour with American style. Baccarat crystal with oversized martinis is one touch of the esthetic taste of this unusual man. With a solid background in gourmandise, with a diploma from the L'Academic Pavillon, with one of the best kitchens in the country, Mr. Masson is fully prepared to tackle the awesome problems that confront restaurateurs in this day and age.

A suitable introduction to the frogpond, an interlude of casual delight and sensual pleasure is lunchtime.

A prix fixe menu is offered — one price covers the complete meal. An interesting beginning at any lunch and one that has long been a favorite at Grenouille is the Choix des hors d'oeuvres. This platter has a wonderful assortment of striped bass with a tangy mayonnaise sauce, tiny, sweet shrimp, pate, celery remoulade and an excellent assortment of marinated vegetables. If you would like a hot appetizer, order the Little Necks Corsini, small clams in a good garlic and butter sauce.

Among the marvelous dishes offered from 13 entrees each evening are a tender and delicious veal Orloff, crisp duck, fillet of beef Perigourdin with a fantastic truffle sauce, and filet of sole. Kidneys and sweetbreads are carefully prepared and are savory dishes.

When you have enjoyed a classic French appetizer and lovely entree, you will behold the most spectacular part of the meal . . . Chocolate souffle. After traveling to thousands of restaurants, I believe this takes top billing as the finest in America. It is rich, sensuous, delightful. This is served with either whipped cream or a Grand Marnier sauce. Sit back with your coffee and bask in the finale of a beautiful evening in Manhattan.

The celebrated wine cellar at La Grenouille lives up to its reputation. Some of the white wines are spectacular and your palate will be pampered in having a good, though not necessarily an expensive, wine with dinner.

A large part of the praise for this restaurant is aimed toward the superb management and well-trained staff. Service can make the difference between an enjoyable meal and a memorable one, and these friendly and meticulous waiters are snappy and "with it." Their tendency toward friendliness rather than arrogance is a definite plus and certainly delight me more than many of the "starched penguins" who march in line in other lauded French restaurants.

For most of us, caviar and foie gras are not everyday occurances. But then . . . along comes a special occasion, and there is no better recommendation from our list than this rare restaurant. It meets our standards in the kitchen, in the service and in the lovely ambience. In all three areas, La Grenouille is a winner.

Now that your mouth is watering, make your reservations well in advance. Don your best finery and watch all the fun-loving and famous diners appear on the scene. The waiters carefully tend and pamper your every want. You may wonder at the relaxed feeling that suddenly sweeps over you, but, after all, that is how it should be. For you are now in the best loved frogpond in America!

Grand Marnier Sauce

from La Grenouille

5 egg yolks	½ cup Grand Marnier
½ cup plus 2 Tbsp. sugar	1 cup heavy cream

Put the egg yolks and about half the sugar in a mixing bowl and beat. Place the bowl over a pan of boiling water and continue beating until the yolks are pale yellow and have thickened. Beat for 8 to 10 minutes.

Remove the bowl from the pan and stir in half the Grand Marnier. Cool. Refrigerate until chilled. When this is cold, beat the cream with 2 Tbsp. of sugar. Beat the cream until it is almost stiff. Fold this into the cold sauce. Stir in the remaining liqueur and blend.

10 servings.

Grotta Azzura

More than half a century ago the Grotta Azzurra, a small family style Italian restaurant, opened for business. The proprietors were John Davino and his wife, an ambitious young couple who had recently arrived from Naples. They left a family who loved to cook and as soon as they could opened a restaurant. Fortunately they passed their recipes on to their children and grandchildren. Today New Yorkers are still crowding into this small informal restaurant . . . one of the best places in the city to savor the robust and tasty cooking of Southern Italy.

The restaurant is now run by Johnny Davino, the grandson of the original owners, who took over several years ago when his father retired. Waiting in the wings is Johnny's 16 year old son who also hopes to enter the business.

Johnny can often be seen working in the small open kitchen at the rear of the restaurant preparing such specialties as Spedini a la romana . . . a bread and mozzarella cheese topped with anchovy sauce or the very popular combination dish of steak, chicken and sausage contadino. It still amazes me when I see so many spectacular dishes being carried out of that tiny, narrow kitchen. But who's to question such success?

Johnny supervises the purchases each morning to make sure that only the best quality vegetables and the freshest fish are purchased each day.

When you arrive Johnny will try to greet you at the door and usher you to your table. A word of warning. Come early. The Grotta has a "no reservations" policy and the line often extends up the steep flight of steps and out into the street. Celebrities, politicians, Johnny's relatives all must wait their turn. It can be worse than your local bank on Friday afternoon so try to arrive before seven or come for lunch when you'll find many Wall Streeters and possibly an empty table.

At your table you will be cared for by one of the efficient tuxedo-clad waiters most of whom have been working at the Grotta since Johnny was a child. Don't let the imitation cave-like decor misguide you. Everything else about this restaurant is first rate.

After you are seated an extraordinary garlic bread is brought to your table. Garlic bread is served all over the country, but here it is different. It's more like eating crisp garlic with a little bread. You must pass it up if you have an important business meeting the next day. But it's unusually simple to make and you can try it at home.

Appetizers are marvelous and almost a meal by themselves. My favorite is the enormous fresh stuffed artichoke that is always overflowing with a delicious mixture of bread crumbs, spices, garlic, capers and olives. In our family everyone insists on his very own artichoke. I never mind as it's a fine way to keep our kids quiet. All those artichoke leaves can keep them involved while I go on to savor some of the Grotta's other great dishes. Other special appetizers worth trying are the baked clams and the steamed mussels smothered with a highly spiced tomato sauce.

The Pasta dishes are splended. Ravioli, lasagne and manicotti are all home made each day. The noodles are rolled out on a marble table in the kitchen and cut with an odd shaped cookie cutter. One taste and you will have no doubts about their origin. If you happen to go for lunch you will see the noodles drying in the open kitchen. At the Grotta there are over 20 different pasta dishes to choose from including spaghetti with a variety of sauces including garlic, oil and anchovies; clam; marinara and mussel ranging in price from $1.75 to $3.00. The generous portions combined with a salad and a glass of wine makes a lovely light meal.

Ordering an entree here is a difficult decision. There are over sixty dishes to choose from. The seafood is as fresh an any place in the City. You can't go wrong with the Striped Bass Grotta Azzurra style ($4.25) which is made with clams, shrimp, mussels and squid. Lobster Fra Diavolo (priced according to size) is also very popular. Another excellent choice for an entree is the veal pizzaiola ($4.00) that is served in a delicious garlicky tomato based sauce. Other main dishes such as veal cutlet parmigiana start at $2.75

Along with the entree you should try one of the Grotta's interesting vegetables such as escarole saute, mushrooms a la marinara and crisp deep fried zucchini. They are so good that recently when some Indian friends visited this country and reminded us that they were vegetarians we whisked them off to the grotta for vegetables and pasta. They still haven't stopped raving about their meal at the Grotta.

There is an adequate selection of Italian and domestic wines to go with your meal. Most can be ordered in half bottles. During the summer months a pitcher of red wine with fruit is served.

After your entree I suggest that you ask for your check and walk off some of the food by going around the block to Cafe Ferrara where you'll find the best Italian desserts in town. However, if you feel that you can't move on (and often I don't) the Italian cheese cake at the Grotta along with their demi-tasse served in a glass with sugar around the rim will certainly not be a disappointment. Johnny's daily selection of market ripe melon is also an excellent choice.

The Grotta is open every day except Monday from noon to midnight and until 12:30 on Saturday. For those who arrive late don't worry about the door being closed on you. Johnny and staff will stay late if necessary for the customers who have been waiting in line. No one is turned away.

Little Italy is an interesting ethnic section with marvelous food shops and where the streets are lined with old tenements with local people sitting outside their buildings on folding chairs. Scattered throughout this neighborhood around the Grotta (about a 10 minute cab ride from midtown) there are at least 10 good Italian restaurants. The people waiting in line at the Grotta could easily walk into any of them and be seated immediately. But they love eating at the Grotta and they don't mind the wait.

Spaghetti with Garlic and Oil

from Grotta Azzurra

1 lb. spaghetti	½ cup olive oil
2 T. chopped garlic	½ tsp. chopped parsley

Cook spaghetti. Meanwhile heat olive oil in a pan and cook garlic until brown. Then add parsley. Add one tablespoon of the sauce to a pot of cooked and drained spaghetti and saute for a minute or two. This will give the spaghetti more flavor. Now pour the rest of the sauce over the spaghetti; mix together and serve.

Serves 2 to 4.

Stuffed Artichokes

from Grotta Azzurra

2 large artichokes
1 cup Italian
bread crumbs
2 tsp. oregano
¼ tsp. freshly ground
pepper
½ tsp. salt

2 anchovies, chopped
4 black olives, chopped
1 T. capers, chopped
2 large cloves garlic,
sliced
1 cup, 2 T. olive oil

Prepare artichokes by slicing off bottom stem and very top of leaves with a sharp knife. Place artichokes in a deep pot. Cover with water. Add a drop of olive oil to the water and parboil for one hour.

Meanwhile mix together the bread crumbs, oregano-pepper, salt and anchovies, olives, capers and garlic. Moisten the mixture with ¼ to ½ of olive oil.

When artichokes are cooked remove from water and turn upside down to drain. Then spread leaves open and pull out the very center portion of the artichoke. Stuff mixture into the center and between the leaves of each artichoke. Top with a few drops of olive oil. Place artichokes in a pan. Pour ¼ cup of olive oil into the bottom of pan and place under broiler for a few minutes until the tops of artichokes are brown. Serve in a dish with some of the olive oil.

Serves 2.

Veal Scaloppine Pizzaiola

from Grotta Azzurra

4 slices veal scaloppine
4 T. olive oil
1 T. garlic, chopped
1 can Italian tomatoes,
   17 oz. size

1½ tsp. salt
½ tsp. oregano
⅛ tsp. pepper

Heat olive oil in a heavy skillet. When the oil is hot add the garlic and cook until brown. Drain the tomatoes and add to pan along with salt, oregano and pepper. Cook for ten minutes under a high flame. In another skillet heat remaining olive oil and cook the veal for a few minutes on each side. Drain oil from the pan with the veal and pour sauce over the veal. Heat together for just a few minutes. (If you overcook the veal it will dry out.)

Serves 2.

Garlic Bread

from Grotta Azzura

8 slices Italian bread
4 tsp. chopped garlic
oregano

1 T. chopped parsley
8 T. olive oil
freshly ground pepper

Place bread in a shallow pan. On top of each slice of bread place ½ teaspoon of chopped garlic, a sprinkle of oregano, a dash of pepper and some parsley. Moisten bread with the olive oil and place in broiler until top of bread is brown.

Serves 4.

Chicken Cacciatore

from Grotta Azzurra

1 chicken cut into 12
   pieces
1 cup olive oil
½ medium onion,
   chopped
2 cups sliced fresh
   mushrooms

2/3 cup white wine
5 slices Italian prociutto
2 T. butter
2 cups chicken broth
1 tsp. parsley, chopped
freshly ground pepper

Brown chicken in the olive oil. When chicken is almost cooked add onion and cook for about five minutes. Then add the mushrooms and cook for another five minutes. When cooked drain oil from the pan. Now add white wine, prociutto and butter to the chicken. Cook for about ten minutes. Add chicken broth, parsley and a dash of pepper. Simmer until sauce thickens (about ten minutes).

Serves 2.

Luchow's

Since the horse and buggy days . . . since 1882 . . . since New Yorkers first began tracking down schnitzel and pfannkuchen, there has been one notable, extravagant, wildly wonderful German restaurant in New York. This faded pink building has grown through the ages, passed down from one owner to another, and all the while there has remained a remarkable consistency in the magical kitchen. A common meeting ground for everyday people and those of fame, Luchow's extends its charm and hospitality to thousands each week who come to feast on the gigantic meals and to delight in the mellow, old surroundings.

Without question, strange and exciting things have happened at this landmark restaurant ever since August Luchow began his modest establishment back in the early 1880's. At one of the famous tables, Gus Kahn composed an all American favorite song, "Yes, Sir, That's My Baby". For years Victor Herbert was maestro over that lovable Viennese string ensemble and today, as in yesteryears, the band plays on.

Lillian Russell is said to have out-eaten her enormous gourmand, "Diamond Jim" Brady (after first politely removing her corset in the powder room!) and the Roosevelts talked politics and world events over their favorite specialties at Luchow's. Despite the atmosphere of a three-ring circus, business was transacted, schmaltzy pleasure was enjoyed, and generations wined and dined in a unique manner.

Today, with all the seriousness of top restaurateurs, the Riese brothers carry on in the marvelous tradition of the original owner. From the enormous, old kitchen come some of the finest dishes in the city. Where else can you get Canadian hare and red cabbage? The mouth-watering fragrances are almost too much to bear. Sweet, tender veal is prepared with dabs of butter, roast suckling pig is an everyday occurance, hundreds of Black Forest mushrooms are cleaned to adorn the celebrated dishes, and tons of beautiful ingredients are being tended with love and care.

Dozens of dishes are available. Cold peach soup is a cooling, delightful beginning for a fabulous dinner. Made with red wine and plenty of cream, this mellow dish is a favorite of mine. Soft-shelled crab mingles with asparagus and hollandaise, and the affinity is beautiful! A superb French chef moves swiftly through the elaborate motions of an artist, and the food continues to pour out in amazing quantities.

Most newcomers to Luchow's are amazed at the grandeur of superb fish dishes — Rocky Mountain trout, Dover Sole, and exquisite salmon. There are dozens of German specialties that are outstanding. Famous Sauerbraten and red cabbage is just the barest beginning. Calf's Liver, Veal Goulash, Schnitzel, or Steak Tartare are prepared to perfection, and if you have difficulty making up your mind, just order "Drei Mignons a la Berliner." This oversized entree includes one pork fillet, one beef, and one veal, and you will have a difficult time choosing the one that is most delicious. Mixed with a rich hollandaise sauce, artichokes and wild rice, this is a buffet in itself!

Christmas is really Christmas at Luchow's! Early in December the staff goes to work setting up one of the largest indoor Christmas trees in the world. This holiday treat is, for children and adults alike, one of the very special holiday outings in the city. Often there are the very youngest of the restaurant goers, smiling in delight along with parents and grandparents.

In the brigade of waiters, you will find some of the finest "characters" in the city. They are terrific. For nearly a century they have encouraged the oh's and ah's over such specialties as Luchow's wonderful soups. Thick, hearty lentil soup, home made noodle soup, consomme, or old fashioned chicken broth with rice delight the palate of many guests.

Enter the enormous dining rooms that accommodate hundreds. A maze of splendid old rooms . . . the Hunt Room, the Nibelungen Room, the central dining room, known as "The Garden" all blend together into mix-matched harmony. The center garden room is the hub of the setting, and it is here that the string quartet seren-ades with all the memories of old Vienna.

This is an ideal place to visit on Sundays when you have time to relax and enjoy the scene. Around your table you are sure to see many guests having the fam-ous German pancakes. These epicurean wonders are about 18 inches across, soon adorned by a well-trained waiter with his luscious assortment of fruits, sugar, cinnamon, and flaming liqueur. Today, you can make the same wonderful pancakes in your own kitchen, but you will never quite capture the glory of all the won-derful years at Luchow's, a great and memorable place to dine in New York since 1882!

Schnitzel a la Luchow

from Luchow's

6 eggs
1 Tbsp. chopped chives
1 tsp. salt
¼ tsp. pepper
10 medium-sized
mushrooms, sliced
4 6-oz. veal cutlets,
about ¼″ thick

8 Tbsp. butter
1 c. beef stock
1 tsp. butter mixed to
smooth paste with 1
tsp. flour
16 stalks fresh cooked
asparagus

Beat the eggs and stir in chives, salt and pepper. Set aside. Wash and slice mushrooms. With a damp cloth wipe veal cutlets. Pound between pieces of waxed paper until very thin. In large skillet heat 4 Tbsp. butter and cook cutlets in it for about 1 minute each side, or until browned. Remove to serving dish and keep warm. To pan add beef stock and cook over high heat until reduced to ½ cup. Swirl in butter-flour paste to thicken sauce. Keep hot. In another skillet heat remaining butter and saute' mushrooms 3 minutes, stirring constantly. Add egg mixture and cook over moderate heat, stirring constantly from sides and bottom of pan, until eggs are barely set. Spoon eggs over cutlets. Streak each serving with a band of the gravy. Garnish with hot asparagus.

Sauerbraten

from Luchow's

3 lb. round steak	½ c. red wine vinegar
1 Tbsp. salt	2 bay leaves
½ tsp. pepper	3½ c. water
2 onions, sliced	2 Tbsp. kidney fat
1 carrot, sliced	4 Tbsp. butter
1 stalk celery, chopped	3 Tbsp. flour
4 cloves	1 Tbsp. sugar
4 peppercorns	5 gingersnaps, crushed

Wipe steak with damp cloth and sprinkle with salt and pepper. Place in a deep bowl and add onions, carrot, celery, peppercorns, wine vinegar, bay leaves and water. Add more water if necessary to cover meat. Cover container and refrigerate 4 days. On fifth day, remove from refrigerator. Drain meat and pat dry with paper towels. Strain and reserve marinade. In heavy casserole heat kidney fat and 1 Tbsp. butter. Add steak and cook over high heat until well browned on both sides. Add marinade, bring to boil, cover and simmer over low heat 3 hours.

Gravy: In small skillet melt remaining butter. Stir in flour and sugar and cook, stirring until roux becomes a dark color, about the color of dark brown sugar. Add to meat liquid, cover, and continue to simmer one hour longer. Remove meat to warm platter. Add to gravy gingersnaps and cook, stirring, until sauce smooth and thickened. Strain into sauce boat and serve with meat slices.

Basic German Pancake

from Luchow's

6 large eggs	1 Tbsp. sugar
1½ c. sifted flour	2 c. milk
¼ tsp. salt	

Beat eggs in large bowl. Beat in flour, salt and sugar. Gradually add milk and beat several minutes. Pour batter into a pitcher or glass measure and let stand for 30 minutes. Any batter not used can be stored covered in refrigerator.

1 Tbsp. butter	Powdered cinnamon
1 jar (14¾ oz.)	Juice of ½ lemon
Lingonberries, heated	¼ c. Jamaica rum or
Confectioners' sugar	kirsch (optional)

In large crepe pan melt butter over medium heat. When butter begins to turn golden, pour in about ½ cup batter. Quickly swirl pan to coat bottom with a large thin pancake. Cook until brown, turn with large pancake turner, and brown on other side. Slip onto hot platter. Sprinkle thickly with confectioners' sugar, cinnamon and lemon juice. Spread with hot lingonberries and roll like jelly roll. Sprinkle with more sugar and cinnamon. If desired, sprinkle with kirsch or rum and ignite. Cut pancake in half for 2 servings.

Apple Pancake

from Luchow's

German pancake batter	1 sliced raw apple
(recipe above)	Sugar
2 Tbsp. butter	Cinnamon

In a large frying pan melt butter and coat bottom and sides. Pour in 3 Tbsp. batter, or enough for very thin coating. Tilt pan to spread batter evenly and cook 1 minute. Cover with apple slices. Pour 3 Tbsp. batter over apple. Turn cake when browned and brown other side. Turn pancake out on a hot platter and fold over or roll loosely. Dash with sugar and cinnamon. Cut in half to serve 2.

Lutece

From his earliest memories at his Mother's side, (she was a spectacular Cordon Bleu) Andre' Soltner has been in the kitchen. In their pleasant home in the picturesque Alsatian town of Thann, young Andre' was fascinated with the culinary activities of the household. His palate for wine was also developing in these early years from his father, a carpenter, who kept barrels of good wine on hand. What better beginning for the owner and chef of one of the best French restaurants in America?

Andre' Soltner is a man whose talents have been noticed for a long time. He worked in restaurants in Paris and Deauville, and was eager to learn wherever he worked. In 1968, he was selected as one of the "Les Meilleurs Ouvriers de France," and there are no loftier heights a chef can aspire to. After working in many of the great European restaurants, this gifted young man now presides in one of the smallest — and best — kitchens in Manhattan. Measuring only 8 by 22 feet, the kitchen at Lutece produces some of the most exciting dishes known to man.

This gracious restaurant impresses me enormously, and despite the rather high prices, huge numbers of knowledgeable gourmands find their way to the quaint, restored town house on East 50th Street. Down a narrow row of stairs, you enter the magical world of Soltner. You are suddenly a part of his world. A tiny bar, a small dining room, upstairs seating or out on the terrace are the choices, but they are all delightful! During summer months the garden room is a mass of trellis walls and wandering ivy, bunches of pink and red begonias, hanging baskets and airy wicker chairs . . . and it all adds up to an intoxicating mood of an elegant summer picnic.

Begin your meal with one of the delicious appetizers on the menu. A good choice is Mousseline de Grenouilles, a light dumpling of pike with frogs legs. You may nibble an excellent quiche, escargots, or sausage encased in a splended brioche. If you want an assortment, order the pate en croute et terrines, four lovely tidbits that "melt in your mouth."

Your sense of well being is heightened by the excellent waiters who are as sincere and anxious for guests to enjoy this tour de force meal as the chef is. Mr. Soltner is not apt to be out front shaking hands, as many restaurateurs do, but he is usually attired in the traditional chef's whites and toque and working with the diligence and love of an artist in his studio.

Main courses are magnificent. The veal dishes are my favorites, often served in an incredible sauce of morrilles. This rare wild black mushroom is a delicacy, and the veal is tender and delicious. Mignon de boeuf in croute is another specialty that is baked in pastry and adorned with foie gras truffles and mushroom puree.

Vegetables, fruits, and salads are handled with artistry and they are a delight to behold. Though the menu is not extensive, I would have to spend a week dining here to fully satisfy my taste buds. Each ingredient that is used is the freshest, most flavorful, and best quality that can be found, and this attention to detail is the secret to the kitchen's greatness.

A $10 bottle of wine can be had that is quite enjoyable. If you were to ask Mr. Soltner, he might recommend a Riesling d'Alsace, which is light and quite suitable to the meal that one is served at Lutece. You don't have to order $40 and $50 wines to enjoy dining out in the finest of the New York restaurants.

Thinking of the desserts at Lutece brings to mind a marvelous, creamy chocolate mousse, a delicate raspberry souffle, or some extravagant pastry such as you have never tasted before. Try Succes a l'Orange, a frozen, layered dessert, which is a mountain of whipped cream, grated orange peel, pastry, and Grand Marnier. What an incredible finale to a great dinner!

This word of advice might be of help to those who have read that a meal for two on any given evening might result in a tab close to $100. My suggestion is . . . "Go for lunch." Though a complete lunch is not cheap, it is worth every penny and will be an experience that you will long remember.

Winner of five gold medals in culinary competition, Andre' Soltner continues to work up to 16 hours a day. His greatest advice to amateurs is to "keep food simple," though his own style is daring and practically unmatched. He readily admits that he wooed and won his wife with his cooking.

It has been said that a chef would rather part with a pint of his blood than one of his cherished recipes. However, this handsome, friendly young chef is no prima donna. He shared with me an assortment of marvelous recipes that I am proud to include in this book and many of the specialties from Lutece will be easy for you to prepare in your own kitchen. As long as dining out in New York's great restaurants continues to be one of the country's favorite pastimes, as long as the dynamic Mr. Soltner presides with such splendor, I urge you to make reservations at this very special restaurant, and when you arrive at Lutece, you have arrived at the top!

Beef Bouillon with Marrow Dumplings

from Lutece

3 pounds soup beef
and bones

2 white turnips,
quartered

2 carrots, quartered

1 leek, sliced

1 onion, sliced

1 rib celery

Few sprigs parsley

1 whole clove

3 quarts cold water

1 T. salt

½ tsp. pepper

Quenelles: (Dumplings)

¼ cup beef marrow (Buy
several marrow
bones)

½ cup packaged
bread crumbs

¼ cup instant flour

1 egg

Dash nutmeg

1 T. chopped parsley

¼ tsp. salt

⅛ tsp. pepper

Place all ingredients for the bouillon in a heavy kettle and bring to boiling. Skim off the scum. Partially cover kettle and cook three hours, skimming when necessary. Strain and reserve the broth.

Make the quenelles by digging out the marrow from the bones. Mash marrow with a fork. Gradually mix the remaining ingredients and form into balls the size of marbles. Roll lightly in flour.

Bring the strained soup to a boil. Add quenelles and poach about 10 minutes over low heat. Serve in soup plates.

Serves 6.

Terrine de Campagne Aux Noisettes

(Country-style Pate' with Filberts)

from Lutece

½ cup whole shelled
  filberts
½ pound pork liver
½ pound boneless
  pork shoulder
½ pound boneless
  veal shoulder
½ pound fresh belly
  pork (unsmoked,
  unsalted bacon)
2 eggs

2 T. flour
1 cup dry white wine
½ cup chopped shallots
2 T. butter
2 tsp. salt
¼ tsp. pepper
½ pound pork fat back
  cut in thin slices
Aspic
Toast triangles
Sour gherkins

Roast filberts in a moderate oven 15 minutes to loosen skins. Rub nuts between towels to remove skins. Grind the liver, pork shoulder, veal shoulder and fresh bacon through the medium blade of a meat grinder two times.

Add eggs, flour and wine to meat mixture. Saute shallots in butter until golden. Add shallots to meat mixture along with salt, pepper and filberts. Mix well.

Line a heavy casserole (with a cover) with the fat back strips. Pack the meat mixture into the casserole. Let stand overnight in a cool place or cover and leave in the refrigerator.

Next day remove casserole and let stand at room temperature one hour. Seal edges with a paste made of 1 cup flour and about 6 tablespoons of water. Set in a pan of boiling water.

Bake in a moderate oven (350 degrees) for 1½ hours. Remove paste seal and cover. Heat ½ cup of hot aspic and pour over meat mixture. Allow the liquid to soak in. Cover and bake an additional 30 minutes. Cool and let set 24 hours before serving. Serve this in thin slices with a garnish of chopped aspic, toast triangles and gherkins.

Makes 8 servings.

Poulet en Croute Lutece

from Lutece

2 packages (10 ounces each) frozen patty shells
1 cup canned chicken broth
2 chicken livers or 1 T. liver pate'
1 small onion, finely chopped
¼ pound mushrooms, very finely chopped
butter
¼ tsp. salt
Dash pepper
1 egg yolk, slightly beaten
2 whole chicken breasts (1¾ pounds)
1 egg yolk
2 tsp. water
Sauce Perigourdine (recipe included)

Remove two of the patty shells from one package. Reseal package and refreeze. Remove all six shells from other package. Let the 8 shells thaw slightly.

Bring chicken broth to boiling in small saucepan. Drop in chicken livers and lower heat. Simmer about three minutes or until pink color is gone. Remove livers with slotted spoon and mash with a fork. Reserve the broth.

Melt butter in skillet. Cook onion and mushrooms until they thicken to a pastelike consistency, stirring continuously. Stir in mashed livers (or pate') salt, pepper and beaten egg yolk. This is the duxelles mixture for stuffing. Heat oven to 450 degrees.

Cut chicken breasts in half and remove rib and breast bones. Put bones in bottom of a butter baking dish. Shape chicken breasts around bones, cupping hands around the chicken to form a compact shape.

Pour ½ cup of the reserved chicken broth around the chicken. Butter a square of foil. Place, buttered side down, over chicken. Poach in preheated oven for 20 minutes and remove from oven. Reset oven to 375 degrees. Lift chicken from bones and cool.

Roll each patty shell to a 5 inch round on a lightly floured pastry board. Place chicken pieces on each of four of the pastry rounds. Spread the duxelles mixtures over the chicken with a spatula. Brush the edges of the pastry with water. Place remaining pastry rounds on top and press edges to seal. Flute edges or tuck under the chicken. Blend remaining egg yolk with water. Brush over pastry. Place on pan and bake 20 minutes or until golden brown. Serve with Sauce Perigourdine.

Serves 4.

Sauce Perigourdine

from Lutece

4 T. sweet butter	1 cup beef broth
(½ stick)	½ cup Madeira
4 T. flour	1 can (⅞ oz.) truffles

Melt sweet butter in medium skillet. Add flour and cook over medium heat, stirring constantly. Cook until mixture turns a light brown. (about 5 minutes)

Slowly add beef broth and continue stirring until thickened. Add Madeira and continue cooking for about 30 minutes, stirring occasionally. When sauce is reduced to about 1 cup, slice 1 can (⅞ ounce) truffles. Add to sauce and heat gently, being careful not to boil. This is excellent served with the wonderful recipe Poulet in Croute from Lutece.

Carrots Glacees

from Lutece

1 pound slender	4 T. sweet butter (½
young carrots	stick)
2 T. sugar	2 cups water
1 tsp. salt	1 T. parsley, minced

Scrape the carrots and cut into 2 inch lengths. Save the very thin ends of the carrots for another meal. Put the carrots in a large saucepan with the sugar, salt, butter and water. Bring to boiling over high heat and then lower flame to simmer. Let carrots simmer, uncovered, 20 minutes or until carrots are tender.

To prevent overcooking . . . if carrots are tender before all the water has evaporated, lift them out with a slotted spoon to a bowl. Continue cooking the liquid in the pan until the water is gone and the clear sugar and butter mixture is left. Return the carrots and cook a minute or two longer until they are glazed. Sprinkle with parsley.

4 Servings.

Tart a L'Orange

from Lutece

1 package (12 oz.) frozen patty shells, thawed	¼ cup flour
	1 tsp. grated lemon rind
6 medium oranges	6 ladyfingers
4 egg yolks	½ cup apricot preserves
1/3 cup sugar	1 Tbsp. sugar
	6 Tbsp. Grand Marnier

Heat oven to 450 degrees. Arrange patty shells in a circle, barely touching, on a floured pastry board; roll the dough out, keeping circular shape to a 12 inch round. Fit the pastry into a 9 inch layer pan with a removable bottom or a 9 inch fluted quiche pan. Turn edges of pastry under and crimp.

Fit a piece of foil into the shell. Fill shell with rice and put into the preheated oven. Turn the heat down to 400 degrees immediately. Bake shell 15 minutes. Remove rice and foil. (Discard) Sprinkle bottom of shell with sugar. Prick lightly with a fork and bake 20 minutes longer, until the pastry is golden and the sugar begins to caramelize. Cool on wire rack.

Grate 1 orange and reserve rind. Squeeze enough oranges to yield 1½ cups juice. Beat egg yolks slightly in top of a double boiler. Beat in sugar and flour and stir in the orange juice. Cook over hot, not boiling, water until very thick. (about 7 minutes) Add orange and lemon rinds.

Split ladyfingers in half. Slice each half lengthwise and in half.

Simmer apricot preserves and the sugar with 2 T. Grand Marnier in a small saucepan for two minutes. Run through a fine sieve. Cool slightly. Slice the two remaining oranges in *paper-thin* slices. Remove seeds. Put on a large plate and sprinkle with remaining 4 T. Grand Marnier. Let stand 10 minutes.

Spoon orange cream into shell. Arrange the slices of ladyfingers over cream to cover completely. Fill in spaces with pieces cut to fit. Drain oranges. Sprinkle ladyfingers with liqueur drained from oranges. Arrange orange slices over ladyfingers, slightly overlapping. (in a circular pattern. Brush oranges and pastry with preserves. Cool slightly and refrigerate.

Serves 8.

Individual Orange Souffles

from Lutece

½ stick sweet butter	1½ cups milk, scalded
½ cup all-purpose flour	5 egg yolks
1/3 cup plus 1½ T. sugar	2 T. Grand Marnier
2 large navel oranges	6 egg whites
	2 T. Confectioners' sugar

Butter 8 small individual souffle dishes. Dust lightly with sugar. Melt butter in a saucepan. Blend in the flour, and continue cooking. Stir constantly for about two minutes. Cool slightly.

Add the sugar to the milk and stir. Whisk the milk mixture rapidly into the roux until smooth. (The butter and flour mixture is called a roux.) Cook and continue to stir until mixture is thickened and comes to a boil. Remove from heat.

Grate rind of oranges and peel and section oranges. Whisk egg yolks, grated orange rind and Grand Marnier into hot mixture. Beat egg whites until stiff and fold into hot mixture.

Fill prepared souffle dishes 1/3 full with mixture. Divide orange sections and add enough mixture to fill each dish three-fourths full. Bake in moderate oven (375 degrees) for 18 minutes or until souffles are puffed and golden. Sprinkle tops with confectioners' sugar and serve at once. If desired the above recipe can be baked as one large souffle.

Serves 8.

Maxwell's Plum

Above you might be eight thousand pounds of leaded Tiffany glass spectacularly arranged in a floral pattern. Below this unusual ceiling European antiques are displayed amidst beautiful hanging plants. Flowers grow in old tile planters. Oversized ceramic animals embellish the walls while Tiffany chandeliers and gas lamps cast a dim light over all. This charming clutter is the backdrop for Maxwell's Plum, one of the city's most popular restaurants.

Eating at Maxwell's is like dining on a set left over from a Broadway extravaganza. It's not at all surprising that the owner, Werner LeRoy, is a producer and director. LeRoy spent two million dollars creating the background for this eating show (the Tiffany ceiling alone cost $260,000) and he is the first to admit that it could never be reproduced.

This Alice in Wonderland like dining spot is located on New York's upper East side. The menu reads Maxwell's Plum . . . restaurant . . . cafe . . . gathering place. And that's what it is. Fortunately LeRoy's dream as a restaurateur was not an impossible one. All he wanted to see was a great cafe restaurant on the East side of Manhattan that was not only a friendly place to eat and congregate but was itself a piece of theatre.

It became a reality in 1966 when Maxwell's opened its doors as a small sidewalk cafe where boy could meet girl . . . hamburgers were heavenly and good drinks were served. As business flourished a more formal back dining room was added. Now it is like a long running show where the seats sell out each evening. Very often it's even difficult to find standing room. Still a fun place to eat and drink, it has today grown into an internationally known restaurant popular with New Yorkers and tourists alike. Take your visitors to Maxwell's and they can continue sightseeing right through their meal. It's a favorite too, among Europeans who think the lively, jumping atmosphere typifies New York.

Diplomats . . visiting dignitaries . . local government officials . . . along with young swingers all head for Maxwell's where the choice varies from chili to cassoulet. Maxwell's is the sort of place where everyone can come as they choose. People flow into Maxwell's in elaborate evening dresses with tuxedo clad escorts. Seated next to them might be a couple wearing washed out jeans. Neither feels the least bit uncomfortable.

In the center of the restaurant is a massive wood paneled bar, long popular with New York's young singles. It's usually crowded. Many are waiting for a table in the romantic glass enclosed sidewalk cafe area, most popular for lunch and informal dining. More serious eaters usually prefer the posh back room. This area attracts the upper eschelon in publishing . . . members of the diplomatic corps and less swingy sorts. Many like the view as it overlooks the bar. Those who retreat to the back may dine on such esoteric fare as roast wild boar and Scotch grouse. Steaks (au poivre, double sirloin, chateaubriand) are also popular.

Some arrive at Maxwell's with only a few dollars in their pocket and a lot of time. That's all right too. A bowl of chili costs only 95 cents. Some of the voyeurs order only a cup of expresso (there is no minimum) and no one bothers them.

There are three slightly different a la carte menus, one for lunch; the others for each of the dining areas in the evening. Prices range from $2.85 for an enormous hamburger to $21.50 for the double sirloin. In between is a huge international menu. I must confess that although I visited Maxwell's many times I have not gotten halfway through the long list of interesting dishes.

As you glance at, or in this case study, the menu you will discover a choice of 25 appetizers . . . pate en croute . . . artichokes served with hot butter or hollandaise . . . smoked trout to name just a few. The chef also makes a well seasoned gazpacho which can be a perfect beginning on a hot summer day. Entrees are even more varied . . . chicken curry . . . marinated spare ribs . . . cannelloni . . . roast duckling normande. Then there is a plat du jour at $5.45 (on Friday it's bouillabaisse). Lighter favorites include the spinach, bacon and mushroom salad, eggs benedict and quiche.

With this take advantage of Maxwell's large wine cellar that has received high marks from many food and wine writers in the city. Most impressive is the good selection of moderately priced wines.

Desserts run the gamut from cheese served with a basket of fruit to an extravagantly rich black forest chocolate cake.

For many, Sunday in New York City is a relatively quiet day. At Maxwell's it's the busiest. There is no formal brunch menu but more of my out of town friends want to brunch here than at any other restaurant in town. I never mind. What could be a better way to begin a Sunday than with a bloody mary, and a choice of thirteen omelettes (from chili to sour cream); ham, cheese and spinach souffle or corn beef hash. Maxwell's considers Sunday family day and your children are welcome. Two youngsters could easily share a hamburger which makes commercial whoppers look a bit undernourished. Whenever you come it is advisable to have a reservation. Be sure to specify where you prefer to sit.

With a menu of such variety one can't help but wonder about the backstage area. I asked the owner how such an elaborate production of dishes can be served each day of the week. This continuous performance is

97

directed by head chef Daniel Fuchs who came here several years ago after working at Quo Vadis. Helping him are two assistants and 26 cooks who work in two shifts. How could there be any less in a restaurant that each month serves 1400 artichokes, 1600 caesar salads and 1,000 slices of black forest chocolate cake. Fuchs begins many a day at 8 a.m. at the meat market where he makes certain everything purchased is of the finest quality. One sure way of judging quality is a restaurant's steak tartar. At Maxwell's it is first rate. When meeting chef Fuchs I expected to see a harried, overworked chef. I was pleasantly surprised to find that he was calm. He even found time recently to win a prize for an artistic buffet from the Societe des Cuisiniers.

Besides eating well you will be cared for by attractive and efficient young waiters who all go through Maxwell's special training course. If some of these handsome lads look familiar, quite possibly you last saw them on a TV commercial or at the theatre.

It's hard to believe that Werner LeRoy and his wife Kay who own Maxwell's along with the Hardwicke Corp. were complete amateurs when they started their restaurant. Today both maintain a keen interest in the operation of Maxwell's. Werner stops by each day while Kay runs this show with the efficiency of a stage manager. One day she might be found at the market selecting fresh vegetables which are later perfectly prepared by the chef. Back in the kitchen, Kay can be found baking tarts tatin.

These one time amateurs are anything but that today. Together they have produced a successful medley of food, atmosphere and people. Whether you're a New Yorker looking for an interesting informal spot to eat or a tired tourist stop off at Maxwell's. It's one of the greatest shows in town!

Quiche Lorraine

from Maxwell's Plum

Pastry

1 1/3 cups flour	1 tsp. salt
1 stick sweet butter	3 T. cold water

Filling

¼ lb. bacon, cut into 1 inch pieces, cooked until crisp	4 eggs
	2 cups heavy cream
	1½ tsp. salt
¼ lb. Swiss cheese, grated	¼ tsp. white pepper
	¼ tsp. nutmeg

Mix flour and butter in a bowl with your fingertips. Add salt and water and knead only until dough is well mixed. Dough should be made 12 hours ahead. Cover with a wet towel and place in the refrigerator.

Roll the dough until it is ⅛ inch thick and line four 4-inch pie pans. Then line the pastry shell with foil and raw beans. Cook the shells in a 325 degree oven for 15 minutes. Discard the foil and beans.

Spread the bacon on the bottom of the half cooked pastry shells. Beat the cream with eggs, salt, pepper, nutmeg and cheese. Pour mixture into pastry shells.

Place in a preheated 400 degree oven for 15 to 20 minutes or until the quiche rises and the top browns. Serve warm.

Makes four servings.

Ham, Cheese and Spinach Souffle

from Maxwell's Plum

4 T. sweet butter
4 T. flour
1½ cups milk
1½ tsp. salt
pinch of white pepper
pinch of nutmeg
3 eggs, separated
½ cup Emmenthaler
   Swiss cheese, grated

½ cup Virginia ham,
   diced
½ cup cooked spinach,
   chopped
4 souffle molds, 4 inches
   in diameter and 2
   inches deep, buttered

Melt butter in a saucepan. Add flour and simmer for 5 minutes, being careful not to let the flour brown. Remove from stove.

Boil milk and slowly blend into the roux until smooth. Bring to a boil and add the salt, pepper and nutmeg. Lower the flame and simmer for 10 minutes. Then stir in the egg yolks, cheese, ham and spinach. Blend thoroughly. Cool.

Preheat oven to 400 degrees.

Beat the egg whites until stiff. Slowly add to the mixture, stirring with an upward motion. Fill buttered molds almost to the top with souffle mixture. Place molds on a hot pastry sheet. This allows the souffles to start cooking from the bottom, permitting them to rise easily. Place in the oven for 20 minutes.

Serves 4.

Spinach, Bacon and Mushroom Salad

from Maxwell's Plum

1 lb. fresh spinach	2 T. red wine vinegar
6 slices bacon, crisply cooked and crumbled	¼ cup olive oil
	½ tsp. salt
¼ lb. large mushrooms, thinly sliced	¼ tsp. pepper

Cut the stems off the spinach and wash the leaves well in cold water. Drain leaves and place in a salad bowl. Add bacon and mushrooms.

Mix together the vinegar, oil, salt and pepper. Pour the dressing over salad. Toss well and serve. Serves 6.

Veal Picatta

from Maxwell's Plum

2 lbs. veal, cut from the loin or filet	¼ lb. sweet butter
	2 T. chopped parsley
1 cup flour	¼ cup lemon juice
½ cup cooking oil	salt and pepper to taste

Season veal with salt and pepper and dredge in flour. Heat oil in a heavy skillet and saute the veal for 10 minutes, turning often.

When cooked remove veal to a hot platter. Drain fat from skillet and melt butter. Then add parsley and lemon juice and mix together. Sauce should be very warm, but not boiling. Pour over veal and serve with white rice. Serves 4.

Black Forest Chocolate Cake

from Maxwell's Plum

Cake

5 eggs
1/3 cup sugar
2/3 cup sifted cake
    flour
2 T. cornstarch

2 T. unsweetened cocoa
2 T. hot melted butter
3 bottles chocolate
    sprinkles, 1¾ oz. size

Cream Filling and Coating

1 quart heavy cream
½ cup confectioners'
    sugar

12 squares semisweet
    chocolate
3 T. kirsch

Chocolate Curls

4 squares semisweet chocolate

Preheat oven to 350 degrees. Grease a 9-inch springform pan with butter and dust with flour.

Combine eggs and sugar in a mixing bowl. Place the bowl in a pan containing hot water and put over a low heat. Cook, stirring continuously for about three minutes. Then beat mixture with a whisk or electric mixer for about five minutes until it becomes thick and creamy.

Mix together the flour, cornstarch and cocoa and sift several times. Then fold these ingredients into the eggs. Now slowly fold in the hot melted butter. Pour into the springform pan and bake for 30 minutes. The cake is ready if the center springs back when pressed lightly with your finger. When cooked remove from the oven and allow it to cool.

To make cream filling and coating, whip the cream. Then fold in the confectioners' sugar. Melt chocolate in a double boiler. Then add one half of the whipped cream. Place mixture over a low heat and beat until creamy. Slowly fold in remaining whipped cream. Set aside.

When cake is cool remove sides of the pan and slice into three layers. sprinkle two layers with the kirsch; cover the top with cream filling and place one layer on top of the other. Place the third layer on top and sprinkle with remaining kirsch. Now coat the entire cake with the remaining filling.

Decorate the top of the cake with chocolate curls (see directions below) and place the chocolate sprinkles on the sides. Chill.

Serves 12.

Chocolate Curls

Melt semisweet chocolate in the top of a double boiler. Spread melted chocolate on a cold cookie sheet with a spatula and place in the refrigerator for about 15 minutes. When the chocolate has just set, scrape the chocolate away from you with the last half inch of a large knife. Continue until all the chocolate has been made into curls.

Orsini's

The brothers Orsini . . . Armando and Elio . . . have created one of the most unusual and charming restaurants in New York. It all began about ten years ago as an expensive little coffee house that Armando dreamed up. There were no formal aspirations to haute cuisine, no fabulous menu, and certainly no background in the restaurant business. Being an architectural engineer, Armando was more familiar with apartment buildings than frying pans, but his little "plaything" moved him from the frying pan into the fire — or to put it another way — into one of the "hottest" restaurants in Gotham!

Before long, in that whimsical coffee house there came a steady clientele, followed by a bonafide kitchen. Their well-to-do friends began having a little pasta along with the excellent desserts and coffee. In the typical gallant Orsini fashion, wines were imported, the jet set was courted, and it all added up to a fashionable establishment. The main dining area is on the second floor, but the fantastic mood begins right when you enter the front door.

Oh, to live in New York and laze away long afternoons at the glorious lunch tables upstairs! What total paradise awaits you when you sweep into the darkened foyer at a quarter to two, sip a drink, and watch the beautiful people parade past.

It has become second nature for lovers of Italian food to satisfy their cravings for the glorious dishes of Milan, or Genoa or Florence in the marvelous old converted building on West 56th Street. Blue and white tiled tables are inviting. Old brick walls add country informality. Huge palms and tiny pottery containers with little dabs of fresh flowers create a mood that makes no pretense at grandeur but rather makes you feel at ease immediately.

105

By night, the restaurant takes on a new personality. Downstairs you may dine in a aura of rich velvets and gilded trimmings. Elaborate service and sophisticated decor, along with the specialties of the house, make this a wonderful place for a seven-course meal.

Begin your dinner with one of the delicious appetizers. An all-time favorite is Mozzarella in Carrozza, and it is creamy and appetizing. Baked clams, scampi Orsini, melon or lobster are available, but if you enjoy antipasto, I recommend that for your starter. Tiny, marinated mushrooms, sardines, and all sorts of crisp vegetables make this a temptation I can't resist.

The old fashioned Italian "Zuppa" has not been forgotten. Minestrone is rich and simmering away in the busy kitchen. You may also order Tortellini in Brocox — dumplings filled with chicken in broth, of Zuppa Spinaci e vova, a steaming spinach soup that is outstanding.

Fettucini is being prepared at your right and left. It is one of the most popular dishes on the menu . . . as good as you will find in the city. All the glories and calories of Italy are exemplified in this incredible specialty. Over twenty pastas are available and they run the gamut from large noodles stuffed with ground steak to flat spaghetti in a delicious, spicy clam sauce, from green noodles, covered with wonderful Italian tomato sauce to the old favorite, Gnocchi. There is no end to the many offerings from the kitchen at Orsini's.

If the pastas don't please your mood of the day, try ordering one of the chicken or beef dishes. I enjoy Pollo Scarpariello, bits of chicken cooked with mushrooms and artichokes in a luscious sauce. Many veal specialties are on the menu, and surprisingly enough, steaks are one of the most popular items available.

Perhaps the greatest excitement on the menu is the fantastic homemade cheese cake. This dessert is one of the best in town and is made with tiny bits of candied fruit and plenty of rich, creamy cheese. Cheesecake experts are abundant in New York, and in a recent magazine survey of the best cheesecake in the city, Orsini's was cited for excellence. If you haven't tried Zabaglione al Marsala, just remember that this was once a coffee house, and the desserts were a major attraction. They still are. Zabaglione is made at your table . . . Marsala wine, rum, and a custard cake that is assembled at your table in a little copper casserole and then spooned into a goblet.

It is natural for restaurant critics to get passionate over food. Something as simple as a delicious hot dog with chili at a drive-in can get our salivary glands going in full motion. A thin slice of prosciutto with melon might stir our passions, and we might well swoon over an exquisite appetizer that pleases our taste buds. Many sensual thrills go through our thoughts and bodies each time we taste a new wine or enter a new restaurant or meet a new chef. Anticipation builds up, then evaluation, anger, disappointment, love and on and on. To us a meal is more than lunch or dinner.

At Orsini's all the senses are pleased. It is a must for any trip I make to New York, for in this glorious restaurant that is one of New York society's favorite spaghetti stops, you enjoy that special flavor of Orsini hospitality . . . invented by a pair of talented brothers who turned a fanciful past-time into one of the most delightful restaurants in Manhattan!

Pollo All' Arrabbiata

from Orsini's

1 3½ pound chicken, cut into small pieces	1 tsp. capers
3 T. oil	½ tsp. parsley
Pinch of rosemary	Salt and pepper to taste
3 cloves of garlic, cut	Pinch of red hot pepper
2 anchovies	½ bay leaf
	6 oz. white wine
	2 oz. vinegar

Cut the chicken into 10 or 12 pieces. Saute chicken in oil and rosemary. When the chicken is brown, add cut garlic and allow the garlic to brown. Drain off the oil and discard garlic.

Add the anchovies, mashed, along with the capers, parsley, salt and pepper, and pinch of hot pepper. Pour in the wine and vinegar and the bay leaf and cover pot. Allow the chicken to cook slowly until tender.

Serves 2.

Fettuccine All' Alfredo

from Orsini's

1 pound egg noodles	4 egg yolks
6 T. butter	6 T. Parmesan cheese
4 T. heavy cream	Salt and pepper to taste

Cook the noodles in salted water and drain when cooked. In a separate pan, melt the butter and stir in the cream. Add cooked noodles and mix well with fork. Stir over flame in chafing dish. Add the Parmesan cheese and mix. Just before removing from the flame, mix the four egg yolks in and rapidly toss. Remove and serve at once.

4 servings.

Pollo alla Margarita

from Orsini's

2 breasts of chicken, boneless	½ cup dry sherry
	4 slices mozzarella cheese
2 eggs, well beaten	3 Tbsp. flour
3 Tbsp. butter	olive oil
¼ cup white wine	Salt and pepper

Coat chicken breasts in flour and then dip them into the beaten egg. Fry chicken in hot olive oil until done. Drain chicken on a paper towel.

In a large pan, melt butter. Add wine and sherry and salt and pepper. Stir ingredients for a few minutes over medium heat. Add the chicken breasts. Place a slice of mozzarella cheese on each piece of chicken. Cover the pan and heat until the cheese melts and the sauce is reduced.

Serves 2.

Paradise

Many New Yorkers never discover the wonderful little places to eat that are hidden among all the specialty food shops around Ninth Avenue in Midtown Manhattan. Most are informal, interesting and inexpensive. During a food shopping expedition to this area of the West Side, lunch can be a pleasant interlude. A favorite place that I often head for is the Paradise on West 41st Street just off Ninth Avenue.

Authentic and delicious Greek cooking comes from the kitchen of this unpretentious restaurant. Whether you dine on one quick dish and a glass of wine or linger for hours and enjoy a full scale Greek feast, enter this Paradise and you will experience a touch of warm Greek hospitality.

In the evening the restaurant is a perfect choice when you wish to dine casually on interesting food at prices that won't leave your pockets empty. It's not too far from Madison Square Garden so you can easily stop by for dinner before going to see the Knicks or Rangers. Better still plan to spend an entire evening here.

While Greek cooks are busy in the kitchen preparing your dinner, relax over cocktails or wine and enjoy the Greek music. The Greeks are notorious for long cocktail hours before dinner. With cocktails it is customary to enjoy the many interesting appetizers. So do as the Greeks and start your meal with an order of cold stuffed vine leaves and those flaky phyllo pastries filled with feta cheese and spinach. If you happen to see a familiar face at the table next to yours while savoring these delicious morsels, don't be surprised. Spiro Skoras used to enjoy dining at the Paradise. Today many Greeks as well as Americans travel across the city to eat moussaka, roast lamb and stuffed vine leaves.

Moussaka, sometimes described as a distant relative of the Italian classic, lasagne, is by far the most popular dish. It's made with layers of eggplant, tomatoes and chopped meat covered with a rich cream sauce and baked until golden. After tasting it you will probably agree that its popularity is well deserved. The recipe is included in this book. Besides being delicious to eat it can easily be made at home. Eat it at the Paradise or prepare it yourself and become a fan of this impressive dish.

On a recent afternoon a friend wanted a sampling of Greek specialties. She was planning a Greek party at home and wished to taste a variety of dishes. We started our lunch with an assortment of cold appetizers including red caviar salad, vine leaves, feta cheese and baby octopus. Following this was a plate of hot specialties (spinach and cheese pie, vine leaves stuffed with chopped meat and topped with lemon sauce, pastitsio, a baked macaroni and naturally, moussaka). The bill for all this which was shared by two of us was slightly over $6.

Greek salad . . . crisp greens, olives, tomato and feta cheese served with an oil and vinegar dressing is delicious. Salad and an order of spinach and cheese pie makes a fine lunch.

Each day from 11:30 a.m. until three the menu features about eight special entrees costing $2.45 that are served with soup, salad and a beverage. The dishes might be baked breast of lamb or pastitsio. Other entrees both at lunch and dinner are priced from $2.95 to $4. The restaurant remains open until 1 a.m. and reservations are necessary only on Saturday evening.

Lamb, the predominant meat eaten by the Greeks is either baked or roasted and served with a vegetable such as eggplant or okra. The waters that surround Greece are filled with a variety of fish which have become an important part of Greek cookery. Broiled porgy, squid in wine sauce and shrimp a la Paradise (baked shrimps smothered with tomatoes and melted feta cheese) are among the fish offered here.

For dessert don't miss Baklava, that chewy sweet delight of phyllo pastry saturated with nuts and honey. Wash it down with a cup of sweet Greek coffee.

A pleasant and leisurely dinner at the Paradise including an appetizer, Greek salad, entree, dessert and coffee for two people should come to under $15 not including wine.

A Greek catering service can also be found at this Paradise. New Yorkers use them for fabulous Greek dinner parties at home. Paradise will deliver hors d'oeuvres, moussaka and baklava for only $5 per person. For moussaka alone the cost is $1.50 per order which is quite reasonable compared to prices charged by east side gourmet and catering establishments. The restaurant will also supply Greek waiters to serve all this good food to you and your guests. If you're in the mood to throw a more elaborate party with Bouzouki music, dancing Greek waiters and perhaps some traditional Greek style plate smashing there's a private upstairs room at the Paradise. Melina Mercouri held her opening night party there when she made her broadway debut. All you must do is bring along your friends. The Paradise will take care of everything else.

John Petrutas and his brother-in-law, Costas Kokis, are the two Greek gentlemen responsible for this lovely establishment. Since 1958 when they purchased the restaurant from the widow of the original owner, they have worked hard to maintain its high standards.

Don't miss browsing through the fascinating stores in this area with barrels of spices from all over the world overflowing onto the street; visit a Greek pastry shop . . . an Italian delicatessen where you'll find great cheese . . . and even truffles. Stop at one of the many outdoor fruit and vegetable stands. And before leaving, pick up grape leaves and phyllo dough and try your hand at some of the interesting dishes served to you at the Paradise.

Taramosalata
(red caviar mousse)

from Paradise

¼ of 8 oz. jar red
  caviar or tarama
  (carp roe)
1 small onion, finely
  grated
1½ cups olive oil

4 slices trimmed white
  bread
½ cup lemon juice
1 package thinly sliced
  brown bread, cut into
  squares

Mash red caviar or tarama and add onion. Add half the oil, a little at a time and beat into a smooth paste. Moisten white bread; squeeze out excess water and break into small pieces.

Continue to beat mixture, adding alternately small bits of bread, olive oil and lemon juice. Taramosalata should be beaten until a light creamy color.

Serve at room temperature spread over squares of brown bread as a canape.

Serves 6 to 8.

Spanakopita

(spinach and cheese pie)

from Paradise

6 T. fresh dill, chopped
½ cup Italian parsley, chopped
¾ cup scallions, chopped
2 packages frozen spinach, 10 oz. size

1 cup olive oil
6 eggs, beaten
1 lb. feta cheese, crumbled
1 cup melted butter
1 lb. phyllo pastry

Cook spinach and squeeze out water and chop finely. Then mix spinach with the dill, Italian parsley and scallions. Add the olive oil and mix well. Next add the eggs and feta cheese.

Butter a large shallow baking dish. Open the package of phyllo pastry; cover pastry not being used with a damp towel to keep it from drying out. Divide the phyllo sheets in half. Place a sheet of pastry in the baking dish. Then brush with melted butter. Continue this with each sheet until half the pastry is used. Then spread spinach mixture evenly over the pastry. Place remaining sheets of phyllo pastry over the spinach mixture, brushing each sheet with melted butter.

Cut into 2 inch squares for hors d'oeuvres or larger pieces (2 by 4 inches) for an appetizer.

Bake for about 30 minutes or until golden. Serve immediately. Or freeze and reheat in a 325 degree oven for 15 minutes.

Makes about 4 dozen hors d'oeuvres.

Shrimp a la Paradise
(shrimp baked with feta cheese and tomato)

from Paradise

1½ lbs. fresh shrimp
1 cup feta cheese, crumbled
½ can tomato paste, 6 oz. size
½ cup canned tomato sauce
2½ cups canned peeled tomatoes, drained
½ tsp. sugar

3 T. olive oil
¼ cup parsley, finely chopped
1 T. dill, finely chopped
1 clove garlic
½ tsp. dried mustard
2½ cups onion, finely chopped
1 cup dry white wine

Heat the oil in a saucepan and add the onion, cooking until light brown. Add the parsley, dill, garlic, sugar and mustard, blending together. Then add the tomato paste, tomato sauce and peeled tomatoes and cook slowly for half an hour.

Clean shrimp and add them to the mixture, cooking for five minutes or less.

Pour the ingredients into a 2 quart casserole and add the wine. Spread the feta cheese over the top and bake in a pre-heated oven at 425 degrees for 10 minutes or until feta cheese is melted.

Serves 4.

Moussaka

from Paradise

2 medium size eggplants
5 T. butter
2 T. olive oil
1½ lbs. chopped lean beef
1 small Bermuda onion, chopped
½ can tomato paste, 6 oz. size

1 large tomato, thinly sliced
6 T. parsley, chopped
¼ tsp. cinnamon
½ cup dry red wine
1½ tsp. salt
½ tsp. pepper
2 egg yolks, medium size

Sauce

4 T. butter
4 T. flour
½ cup light cream
1 cup milk
½ tsp. salt

¼ tsp. nutmeg
1½ egg yolks, beaten
¼ cup bread crumbs
¼ cup Parmesan cheese

Cut the eggplants into slices about ½ inch thick. Heat 1 T. of the butter and 1 T. of olive oil in a heavy skillet and cook eggplant until just tender. Remove eggplant from the skillet and set aside. Add another tablespoon each of butter and olive oil to the skillet; heat again and cook meat until brown. Set aside.

In another skillet heat 3 T. butter and cook chopped onion until a golden brown color. Then add onions and butter to the skillet with the meat. Mix well. Then add tomato paste, chopped parsley, a heaping ¼ tsp. cinnamon, red wine, salt and pepper. Mix together and cook until the liquid has been absorbed by the meat.

Set the skillet aside. When mixture is cool add the 2 beaten egg yolks, combining them well with the other ingredients.

Heat 4 T. butter in a saucepan. Add flour and mix well. Cook for a few seconds, stirring until butter and flour are well blended and lightly cooked. Remove from heat and add light cream and milk. Stir with a whisk. Then return to heat and cook until sauce thickens, stirring continuously. Remove from heat. Add ½ tsp. salt, ¼ tsp. nutmeg and 1½ beaten egg yolks. Combine egg yolks rapidly with a whisk.

Preheat an oven at 375 degrees.

Butter a shallow baking pan. Sprinkle the bottom with some of the bread crumbs and Parmesan cheese. Then add a layer of eggplant, some tomato slices and then a layer of meat. Sprinkle well with bread crumbs and grated parmesan cheese. Repeat layering until all the ingredients are used up. Pour sauce over the top spreading to cover evenly.

Bake for 35 to 45 minutes or until all is bubbly and top is golden brown.

Serves 6.

Dolmades Avgolemono

(Meat filled vine leaves with lemon sauce)

from Paradise

1 jar grape leaves, 1 lb.	1 T. dried mint leaves
	1 tsp. parsley, chopped

1 lb. ground lamb
¼ cup uncooked rice
1 onion, finely chopped
2 eggs
2 T. butter
2 T. olive oil

1 cup plus 2 T. water
salt and freshly ground
  pepper
3 egg yolks
juice of one lemon

Drop grape leaves into boiling water and drain immediately in a colander. Then combine the ground meat, rice, onion, 2 eggs, half the butter, half the olive oil, mint, parsley, 2 T. water, salt and pepper.

Place a few grape leaves, shiny side down on a flat surface. Put a tablespoon of stuffing in the center of each leaf. Fold over bottom stem, then sides and roll the leaves tightly to enclose the stuffing. If leaves are small or broken put two leaves together.

When all the filling is used there should be some left over leaves. Arrange these leaves over the bottom of a casserole. Place the folded leaves in layers over these leaves. Add the remaining butter, oil and the cup of water.

Cover casserole with a plate that fits directly on top of stuffed leaves. Then cover the casserole. Cook about 30 minutes. Arrange the stuffed grape leaves on a hot dish and pour the hot liquid from the casserole into a measuring cup.

Beat the egg yolks with the lemon juice over a very low flame. Do not cook. Immediately add the hot liquid, beating constantly until sauce is lightly thickened. Do not boil or it will curdle.

Pour the hot sauce over the stuffed leaves and serve hot as an appetizer or light supper entree.

Serves 12.

Le Perigord Park

It's a fact that New York City contains a galaxy of French restaurants . . . from neighborhood bistros to super elegant eateries. The local telephone directory, which is far from complete, lists 85 French restaurants. Choosing a great one to dine at can be difficult, especially to the neophyte. One that we enjoy time and again is Le Perigord Park . . . a handsome restaurant which has the exquisite food and elegance of New York's finest French restaurants at somewhat lower prices.

Sitting over coffee one morning, Willy Kraus, a co-owner of Le Perigord Park, reminisced about how it all began. He recalled an almost insurmountable challenge that had to be overcome in establishing his restaurant in New York. Five years ago when Le Perigord Park opened its doors the need for a new French restaurant in New York City was about as great as for another one in Paris. But that did not stop Monsieur Kraus.

Kraus had everything working for him and if anyone could interest New Yorkers in haute cuisine it had to be he. An ambitious and imaginative young restaurateur, Kraus started his career at a young age in his grandfather's kitchen in Corbil, a Paris suburb. Later he worked in excellent restaurants in Paris and London before arriving in New York. His New York City schooling included Le Pavillon and La Grenouille. While working as executive chef at La Grenouille he met his present partner George Briguet who was the captain. Together they took over Le Perigord in 1965. But this was only the beginning for these entrepreneurs. Four years later they opened Le Perigord Park, a more formal and ambitious establishment.

At Le Perigord Mr. Kraus had worked mainly in the kitchen. Now at his newer restaurant he oversees the entire operation. Under his supervision close attention is paid to every detail.

The restaurant's menu immediately sets it apart from the typical French menus seen over and over in New York. The dishes served are outstanding with excellent specialties . . . marvelous sauces and irresistable desserts. It is interesting to note that escargots do not appear on the menu. Neither did chocolate mousse until recently when Mr. Kraus succumbed to the pressures of his clientele and added it to the dessert list. Kraus would have preferred to stick with a more exotic praline mousse. For customers who dine here often, and there are many that do, Kraus is always present to suggest variations of dishes that appear on the menu just to be sure there are no jaded diners.

In command of the kitchen is the talented Guy Picard, a Cote Basque graduate who does a magnificent job. For beginners his delicate cold striped bass served with a tasty remoulade sauce is exceedingly good and so is the mousse of sole prepared with two remarkable sauces . . . white wine and lobster. Soups are delicious too, especially the lobster bisque. Outstanding entrees include Medallion Prince Orloff . . . tender veal cooked with puree of mushrooms, foie gras, slices of truffles in an excellent cream sauce and turbot poche in a sauce venitienne, a wonderful blend of hollandaise, white wine, chives, parsley and chervil.

With the desserts, Mr. Kraus' careful planning is again evident. Pastries are all baked at the restaurant each day by a first rate pastry chef. Each dessert is a star attraction difficult to bypass. Even if you feel as though you can't consume one more morsel of food your resistance weakens when the dessert cart is rolled before you. Deciding between such delectable choices as raspberry mousse, floating island or one of the fresh fruit tarts (at least three kinds are available each day) will be difficult. Your waiter will probably not allow you to suffer and most often offer you a sample of several desserts.

Talent and experience has worked well to establish Le Perigord Park on the New York restaurant scene. Staying on top is not always an easy job and Kraus often drops by his competitors' restaurants to observe their operations. As we talked about his restaurant, the staff was scurrying about getting ready for the busy day ahead. Yellow roses (to match the decor) were being carefully arranged in brandy snifters for each table in the elegant main dining room as well as for the two smaller more intimate rooms with their attractive curved stucco ceilings. It was dreary and cold outdoors that day, but inside the cheery yellow decor, fragrant fresh flowers and pretty murals adorning the walls brightened things considerably.

At lunch time the restaurant will be filled mostly with publishing and advertising executives who have bid goodbye to the noisy business area for the quiet elegance of 63rd Street and Park Avenue where Le Perigord Park is located. They know that here they will enjoy a leisurely and special lunch which is also one of the best buys in town.

The lunch menu while not as extensive as at dinner is interesting enough. There is always a daily luncheon specialty such as volaille pochee . . . chicken served with a sauce supreme. In all there are about 12 entrees to choose from. During the summer an elegant table of cold specialties is a favorite at lunch. The prix fixe lunch is $9. This includes an appetizer or soup, an entree and dessert (the same super selection as at dinner).

123

It is in the evening that the kitchen really shows off its brilliance. Now there are 18 entrees to choose from including a nightly specialty which could be filet of beef perigourdine (the most popular) or Le cuisseau de veau . . . veal bathed in a sauce of cream, tarragon and mushrooms. The cost of dinner depends on the price of the entree ordered. This ranges from $14 to $16. Wine and drinks of course add to the cost. The wine list is not large but there are several enjoyable wines to be had.

The restaurant is open for lunch on Monday through Friday from 12 until 3 p.m. and dinner is served every day from 6 to 11 p.m. Le Perigord Park is also one of the few fine French restaurants where you can hold a private party and dazzle your guests with haute cuisine.

Looking pleased, Mr. Kraus remarked that Le Perigord Park has become a real New Yorker's restaurant. Tourists rarely come here. They prefer the less formal sister restaurant, Le Perigord on East 52nd Street.

At Le Perigord Park both lunch and dinner are a truly enjoyable adventure in fine dining. Phone in advance for reservations and follow the path to Kraus' door for French cuisine not to be missed in New York. Now, thanks to Mr. Kraus and his fine chef you can also make some of the kitchen's imaginative dishes and have a fabulous French meal at home. Bon appetit.

Escalope de Veau Orloff

from Le Perigord Park

12 thick veal scallops
½ lb. mushrooms,
   finely chopped
2 cups heavy cream
4 T. butter
2 T. vegetable oil
salt and white pepper
¼ tsp. lemon juice
pinch of nutmeg
¼ cup flour
1 egg yolk
2 T. brandy
4 thin slices black
   truffles
2 T. foie gras, diced

This dish is not only rich, but delicious. It would be elegant at a dinner party.

Cook the finely chopped mushrooms in 2 T. butter until the moisture evaporates. Add 1 cup heavy cream and cook for 15 minutes. Season with salt, white pepper, lemon juice and nutmeg. Set aside.

Season veal with salt and white pepper and dust with flour. Melt remaining butter and oil in a heavy skillet and cook the veal for about eight minutes. When cooked arrange veal on a warm ovenproof platter.

Eliminate the fat remaining in the skillet. Add brandy to the pan and deglaze. Then add 1 cup heavy cream, letting it reduce for several minutes. Stir in the egg yolk.

Place the cooked mushrooms on top of the veal. Top with the diced foie gras and truffles. Pour sauce over the scallops and place in the broiler to glaze for about a minute.

Serves 4.

Le Poulet Poele Perigourdine

from Le Perigord Park

1 3 lb. chicken
6 thin slices black
    truffles
1 slice lard
1 onion, sliced
1 carrot sliced
bouquet garni (1 sprig
    parsley, 1 bay leaf, ¼
    tsp. thyme tied in
    cheesecloth)

1 cup Madeira
1 cup brown sauce
½ cup butter
½ cup vegetable oil
2 T. foie gras, diced
salt and freshly ground
    pepper

Insert 4 slices truffles under the skin of the chicken breast. Rub the bird with salt and pepper. Then truss it. Cover the breast with the slice of lard. Wrap the bird loosely in buttered paper or aluminum foil and refrigerate it for a few hours so that the perfume of the truffles permeates the chicken. Dice remaining truffles and set aside.

When ready to cook remove the paper and lard around chicken. Place the chicken on its side in a large casserole. Melt butter and mix with oil. Pour half of the mixture over the bird. Cook the chicken over a moderate heat until it is brown on one side (about 15 minutes). Baste frequently with remaining oil and butter. When brown turn chicken and cook it on the other side for 15 minutes. Then add onion and carrot slices and bouquet garni to the casserole. Turn the chicken and brown remaining sides, cooking about 15 to 20 more minutes. Continue to baste.

When the chicken is cooked and well browned, remove it to a hot serving platter and keep it warm. Re-move fat from the casserole. Add the Madeira and re-duce it allowing the alcohol to evaporate. Then add the brown sauce and bring to a boil. Strain sauce. Add diced truffles and foie gras. Pour sauce over chicken and serve very hot.

Garnish with braised celery and roast potatoes.

Serves 2.

Mousse de Sole Aux Deux Sauces

from Le Perigord Park

2 lbs. filet of Dover sole (Gray sole may be substituted)	¼ tsp. nutmeg
	2 egg whites
	2 cups heavy cream
½ tsp. salt	1 souffle dish, 1½ qt.
¼ tsp. pepper	size, buttered

Cut fish filets into small pieces. Place half of the fish at a time in a blender with a small amount of cream. Blend at a high speed until smooth. When fish is finely ground, reduce the speed and add the seasonings and egg whites. Then, gradually add the remaining heavy cream.

Spoon mixture into a souffle dish. Place souffle dish in a shallow pan filled with hot water and cook in a 350 degree oven for 20 minutes.

When cooked, remove mousse from the mold to a heated platter. Cut into individual servings. Pour a white wine sauce on one side and creamed Lobster Sauce on the other side. Serve immediately with rice.

Serves 6 to 8 as an appetizer.

Lobster Sauce

from Le Perigord Park

claws and tail of 4 lb.
lobster
salt
cayenne pepper
¼ cup brandy
1 T. butter
1 tsp. flour
3 T. vegetable oil
1 carrot, diced
1 medium sized onion,
diced

2 shallots, minced
1 clove garlic, peeled
1 bouquet Garni (3
sprigs parsley, ¼ tsp.
thyme and 1 bay leaf
tied together in
cheesecloth)
2 T. tomato paste
2 cups dry white wine
1 cup fish stock
¼ cup heavy cream

Cut tail and crack claws from a four pound lobster. Reserve the coral (or roe). Sprinkle the claws and tail with salt and cayenne and cook the pieces in hot oil until the shells are red.

Add carrot, onion, shallots, garlic and bouquet garni to the pan. Cook for five minutes. Add tomato paste. Then add ¼ cup heated brandy and ignite. Add white wine and fish stock and cook for 15 minutes.

Strain liquid and add heavy cream. Allow it to reduce for five minutes.

In a small saucepan combine 1 tablespoon butter with 1 teaspoon flour. Add the reserved roe. Use this to thicken the sauce.

Serve over Mousse de Sole.

White Wine Sauce

from Le Perigord Park

6 T. butter	2 T. chopped mushrooms
1 T. flour	½ cup heavy cream
1½ cups fish stock	salt and white pepper
1 cup dry white wine	to taste
2 shallots, chopped	few drops of lemon juice

Mix 2 tablespoons of butter with flour in a saucepan. Make a roux by cooking mixture for a few minutes over a low heat (Do not allow it to brown).

In another saucepan combine fish stock, wine, shallots and mushrooms. Cook mixture until it is reduced by half. Then strain and add the roux to the liquid. Cook, stirring continuously until the sauce is slightly thickened. Add heavy cream and cook for ten minutes.

Season sauce to taste with salt and white pepper, a few drops of lemon juice and as much of the remaining butter as you need.

Serve over Mousse de Sole.

Note: Mousse de Sole is delicious with white wine sauce alone.

Striped Bass
Froid Sauce Remoulade

from Le Perigord Park

1 6lb. striped bass, cleaned
6 oz. wine vinegar
1 onion, sliced
1 carrot, sliced
1 tsp. salt
½ tsp. crushed peppercorns
1 sprig parsley
1 bay leaf
¼ tsp. thyme
1 cucumber, peeled and sliced
6 T. salad oil
2 T. vinegar
1 lemon
cheesecloth

Sauce Remoulade

2 egg yolks
1½ cups salad oil
1 T. wine vinegar
salt and white pepper to taste
1 tsp. Dijon mustard
1 hard boiled egg, chopped
3 sprigs parsley, chopped
1 T. gherkins, chopped
1 T. capers, drained and chopped

In a fish poacher or large shallow pan place 2 qts. water, 6 oz. wine vinegar, onion, carrot, 1 tsp. salt, crushed pepper and bouquet garni (made by placing parsley sprig, bay leaf and thyme on a piece of cheesecloth and tying it together). Boil the mixture for 30 minutes.

Meanwhile, place sliced cucumbers in a dish. Cover with a mixture 6 T. salad oil and 2 T. vinegar and set aside in the refrigerator.

To make sauce put egg yolks, ½ T. of vinegar, mustard, salt and pepper in a large bowl. Beat with a wire whisk for about a minute. Add the oil slowly (one drop at a time), beating continuously until all the oil has been used up. Thin with remaining vinegar if necessary. To this add the hard boiled egg, parsley, gherkins and capers. If you wish 1 tsp. each of chopped tarragon and chopped shallots or chives may also be added.

Now place the striped bass on a piece of cheesecloth and gently lower into the large shallow pan. (The cheesecloth is unnecessary if you use a fish poaching pan). Add additional water to cover fish if needed. Simmer fish gently for 30 minutes. Allow it to cool in the water. Carefully lift fish from the pan. Remove the skin and dark part of the fish.

Arrange fish on a serving platter with slices of cucumber, lemon slices and parsley. Serve remoulade sauce with the fish for an elegant and delicious appetizer.

Serves 4 to 6.

Serves 6 to 8 as an appetizer.

Raspberry Mousse

from Le Perigord Park

½ qt. heavy cream
3 cups sugar
4 egg yolks
5 oz. raspberry Jam
¼ tsp. raspberry extract

2 10 oz. containers,
    frozen raspberries,
    drained
1 oz. kirsch
1 drop red food coloring

Dissolve sugar in 2 cups of water and cook quickly until mixture reaches 240 degrees. Then slowly pour it into a mixing bowl containing the egg yolks. Beat until the mixture is cool and has doubled in volume. (It should be thick and creamy). Add raspberry jam, extract and a drop of food coloring. Beat again for about a minute. Set mixing bowl over ice to keep cool.

Beat cream. When it is about halfway beaten add kirsch and then continue beating until whipped.

Add raspberries to the yolk and sugar mixture. Then add the whipped cream and mix well.

Chill for 1 hour.

Serves 10.

Note: Ingredients in a mousse should be cold. In the summer, cream should be placed in a freezer before beating.

Raspberry extract is made by Wagner's, Ivyland, Pa. 18974. It can be purchased in New York at Balducci's, 424 Sixth Avenue.

Quo Vadis

Restaurant critics continually list Quo Vadis as one of "the 10 best restaurants in New York." And it doesn't take a food expert to recognize the sterling qualities of this famous restaurant. Since 1946, the amazing chefs and talented owners have taken time and patience to keep the exalted reputation untarnished. In a world of changing chefs, closing competitors, new restaurants appearing on the scene, this elegant eatery has maintained a masterful calm and consistent pattern of excellence.

One of the most distinguished Gallic restaurants anywhere in the country, Quo Vadis has a sparkle and style that is quite apart from the numerous high-priced French restaurants that dot Manhattan. A simple pleasure is the absence of darkness. You can both read your menu and see what you are being served.

When you enter the spacious, airy dining room, you are sure to be impressed by the attractive surroundings. Huge paintings, cheerful arrangements of fresh flowers, crisp linen, and comfortable seating make this a delightful place to spend a leisurely evening. Owners Gino and Bruno are a gracious pair of hosts who do everything possible to insure the pleasures of their guests.

The professional service is one of the strong suits at Quo Vadis. A staff of professional waiters, long a part of the wonderful "landscape" translate items from the menu into everyday language. Their recommendations are helpful and interesting . . . anything from eel in green sauce to apricot souffle!

If you glance around at a nearby table, you are apt to see the skillful waiter, deftly slicing a gorgeous filet mignon into juicy, pink slices. Beef knows no finer home than Quo Vadis. It has long been known that the restaurants get first choice of America's finest beef, and when you dine here, you will be well aware of the prime quality of all the beef dishes. Ditto for all the fresh ingredients that go into the preparation of many exciting recipes.

An outstanding dish to sample from this memorable kitchen is soup. Petite Marmite is a glorious choice and there is a whole history to the recipe for this classic delicacy. In France, Petite Marmite is the name of the earthenware pot that has been used for centuries to cook this flavorful dish. It is one of the most delicious soups known to man, robust with the wholesome flavor of chicken, beef, fresh vegetables, and much loving care.

While you are sipping soup, the sauciers and pastry chefs are scurrying around the well-stocked kitchen, filling orders for Crepes Quo Vadis, (highly recommended) oysters au gratin, or escargots. These are just a few of the appetizers that are steaming hot and delicious.

The large ala carte menu offers a dazzling array of seafood, and that is what I am most apt to order. Lobster, oysters, sole, turbot, red snapper, crabmeat, shrimp . . . all appear in dozens of fabulous dishes. Like the best restaurants in New Orleans, this knowledgeable kitchen is expert at preparing a lovely, simple broiled fish. This, to me, is simplicity at its finest . . . just the delicate lemon and butter sauce, with the slightest touch of seasonings.

Exquisite vegetables are cooked just the briefest time possible and tossed with creamy butter and mild seasonings. Broccoli, carrots, artichokes, asparagus . . . all are carefully prepared and beautifully presented. Pigeon, duck, and exquisitely tender veal appear in the classic dishes befitting a top French restaurant.

Food lovers can enjoy the first chilly days of autumn

by visiting Quo Vadis on a Saturday afternoon and sampling Bollito Misto. This elegant dish is an Italian version of the New England boiled dinner and is one of the heartiest dishes in the city.

The chefs "roll up their sleeves" early in the day and begin the elaborate preparation which includes an assortment of fresh vegetables and herbs, veal, boiled beef, chicken, and a zesty Italian sausage. With careful attention, they assemble this magnificent meal and roll it out . . . with an array of accompaniments such as horseradish sauce, Italian mustard fruits, or a tangy vinaigrette sauce.

When your meal is completed, ask to see the dessert cart. On a three-tiered wagon, you will see a dozen marvelous and tempting desserts. Some are as frilly as a lace doily . . . some as bland as a perfectly baked apple. The recipe for Chocolate Mousse is included for you to try at home and is very easy to prepare.

Pamper yourself with a truly memorable evening of dining . . . for fine foods, good company, and lovely wines are an art form unto themselves. As James Beard has written, "Quo Vadis is to me a paragon among New York restaurants, a place of beauty, quiet and comfort." It can be said no better!

Carre d'Agneau Nicoise
(Rack of Lamb)

from Quo Vadis

3 2-lb. racks of lamb
(seven ribs each)

Salt and freshly ground
pepper to taste

1½ cups coarsely
chopped carrots

¼ cup chopped parsley

1 onion, finely chopped

1 tsp. chopped
rosemary

½ cup chopped celery

1 cup chicken broth

¾ cups fresh bread
crumbs

½ cup finely chopped
shallots

½ cup finely chopped
parsley

½ tsp. fresh or dried
thyme

Have the racks of lamb neatly trimmed, French style. Preheat the oven to 500 degrees. Sprinkle the meat all over with salt and pepper. Put the lamb, fat side down, in a large, flat baking pan. Place in the oven for 8 to 10 minutes. When the meat starts to brown well, turn the racks over, fat side up. Continue baking, turning occasionally, allowing about 20 minutes. Reduce the oven heat to 400 degrees.

Pour off the fat in the pan. Scatter the chopped carrots, parsley, onion, rosemary, thyme, and celery around the meat. Cook about 10 minutes longer and add the broth. Cook for an additional 5 minutes.

Pour off and save the broth from the pan. Strain it and keep it hot. Discard vegetables. Place the racks of lamb, fat side up. Make a mixture of bread crumbs, shallots and parsley. Coat the tops of the racks of lamb with the mixture, patting so that it will adhere. Run the lamb quickly under the broiler. Slice and serve hot with the strained broth.

8 to 10 servings.

Steak Diane

from Quo Vadis

1 12-oz. sirloin steak	2 tsp. minced parsley
2 Tbsp. butter	½ tsp. Worcestershire
1 tsp. finely chopped	sauce
shallots	1 Tbsp. A-1 sauce
1 tsp. minced chives	Salt and freshly ground
	pepper to taste

Trim all fat from the steak. Pound steak evenly between two sheets of waxed paper to prevent breaking the meat. Pound until it is very thin. Sprinkle the meat well with salt and pepper.

In a chafing dish, melt one tablespoon of the butter and saute shallots in it. Add the steak, sear it quickly on both sides and add more salt and pepper as desired. Remove the steak to a serving platter.

Melt a tablespoon of butter in the pan juices. Add chives and cook for a few seconds. Add Worcestershire sauce and A-1 Sauce. Blend well and cook until the mixture thickens. Do not boil. Return the steak to the pan. Sprinkle with parsley on each side. Place steak on serving dish and pour the sauce over it.

Serves 1.

Crepe Quo Vadis

from Quo Vadis

1 recipe crepes	6 Tbsp. flour
½ cup cooked shrimp, diced	1 cup milk, heated
	½ cup cream, heated
½ cup lobster, diced	Salt and pepper
1 cup scallops, chopped	Dash of curry powder
½ cup crabmeat	2 egg yolks
5 Tbsp. butter	5 Tbsp. whipped cream

Melt the butter in a saucepan. Slowly add the flour, stirring until smooth. Heat the milk and cream in a separate pan and add very slowly. Stir constantly. When the sauce thickens, add the curry powder, salt, and pepper. Cool slightly. Blend the sea food with about three-fourths of the sauce. (Set aside about ½ cup of plain sauce for use later.)

Divide the sea food mixture between the crepes, putting about 2 Tbsp. in the center of each crepe. Roll up. Place the crepes on a buttered baking pan. Set the oven at 400 degrees and bake.

Beat the egg yolks. Slowly add the plain cream sauce into the eggs. Fold in whipped cream. Spread this mixture on the crepes. Place under the broiler for about two minutes. Serve at once.

Chocolate Souffle

from Quo Vadis

½ cup milk	2 Tbsp. butter
4 heaping Tbsp. sugar	1 tsp. sugar (to sprinkle
4 heaping Tbsp. cocoa	in souffle dish)
4 eggs, separated	pinch of salt

Blend the milk, sugar, and cocoa in a saucepan. Cook slowly until it reaches a boil, stirring constantly. Lower fire and continue cooking until the mixture is thickened. (about 10 minutes) Remove from flame and add egg yolks. Add the butter and beat until you have a smooth batter.

In a separate bowl, beat egg whites with a pinch of salt until you have a firm snow. Using a spatula, slowly fold the whites into the chocolate mixture. Pour into a lightly buttered and sugared souffle mold.

Preheat oven to 350 degrees. Place souffle in the oven and bake for 17 minutes. May be served with Vanilla Sauce or sweetened whipped cream.

Serves 4 to 6.

Romeo Salta

One of the indubitably great culinary masters of Italian cooking in America is a charming, talented man whose restaurant bears his name . . . Romeo Salta. His presence is felt in the expert management of a superb restaurant, but, perhaps even more so to the thousands of "friends" who use his well-known book, "The Pleasures of Italian Cooking." Many of these fans who live too far away to taste the delicacies of Northern Italian tour de force first hand take pleasure in becoming acquainted with Romeo Salta in this popular book.

In that marvelous old restored brownstone, Romeo takes center stage in delivering an exciting assortment of delicious and authentic dishes. He is a perfect host.

Since 1953, the friends of Romeo have delighted in the enormous cooking talents of this noble restaurant. Enter the restaurant with a hearty appetite, for there is no other way to do justice to the meal that you will be served. Large, heavy beams and rough textured walls created a rustic and comfortable setting. The immaculate kitchen is visible from most of the tables, and a staff of expert chefs take great pride in carrying on the traditional dishes that are hundreds of years old.

Friendly waiters take your order, keen on pleasing. Their manner is rather casual and seems fitting for this type of restaurant. They are quick to offer suggestions for a mouth-watering specialty that is soon cooking in the busy kitchen. While you are waiting, you might ask to see the spectacular old Victorian drawing room upstairs. What a sensational place for a private party!

After a drink or two, you will begin one of the most memorable restaurant experiences in the city. From the marvelous array of hors d'oeuvres listed on the menu, you may choose tiny baked clams or mussels, thinly sliced Italian ham, pepper with anchovies, or a classic Antipasto. The latter is sufficient for four, so plan to share it with someone else. Eggplant may be served hot, stuffed with a grand mixture of capers, oregano, and anchovies or it may be prepared with a tomato sauce and served cold. Either way, an everyday vegetable becomes noteworthy.

Zuppa! Most Americans think of Minestrone as the only Italian soup. Not so. At Romeo Salta's there is a wide variety . . . macaroni and bean soup, chicken dumplings in a flavorful broth . . . or fresh spinach soup. Zuppa di Spinaci is a magical blend of cooked spinach, rich broth, ground pepper and tons of cheese. Served with thin, crunchy bread sticks or fresh Italian bread, this is one of the treats of the meal.

A long time specialty of the house is "Straw and Hay." This dish is widely imitated, but no restaurant can outdo this old family recipe. It combines white and green noodles, baked in a casserole with chunks of tender chicken, fresh peas, a creamy sauce and freshly grated parmesan cheese. Splendid! Scampi alla Griglia Romeo is another favorite here made from enormous shrimp, dipped into olive oil, rolled in crumbs and broiled until golden brown. The succulent sauce is a tangy blend of mustard, tomatoes, grated carrots and just the right seasonings.

American shrimp are smaller than true prawns, so this fine restaurant imports scampi. Because of the long coastlines of Italy fish is a plentiful and delicious resource for chefs of that country. Baked trout, fish stew or lobster Diavola are good examples of the talents of the chefs.

If this is your first visit, you will do well to order Cannelloni . . . carefully stuffed with well-seasoned meat. Fettucine lovers are in sheer ecstacy with the creamy dish that is the favorite of many who frequent this well loved restaurant. You haven't tasted spaghetti until you try it with veal dumplings . . . or white clam sauce . . . or plain old terrific tomato sauce.

And then there is manicotti, gnocchi, and the dish Americans most imitate at home . . . or try to . . . lasagna! Add to this a bottle of Chianti, or Verdicchio, or Strega, and you will have visions of another world . . . Italian cuisine equal to the best you will find anyplace in America.

Desserts are superb. One dish that I adore is Torta Mascarpone. This is one of the great Italian desserts in Manhatten . . . layers of chocolate and cheese, orange liqueur, cake, and mountains of fluffy whipped cream. If you are ambitious, you can make this dessert from his recipe.

Centuries after Shakespeare's famous character uttered that immortal line . . . "Wherefore art Thou, Romeo?" I find myself muttering the same words. When the urge strikes me to prepare an Italian banquet, I begin by rambling through the hundreds of cookbooks lining my kitchen shelves until I arrive at that well-worn book by Romeo Salta. In a matter of minutes, that wonderful fragrance of true Italian cooking permeates the air. But if you are in New York, you can do it the easy way. Hop in a cab, head for West 56th Street, and dine with the Maestro . . . Romeo Salta!

Fillet of Beef Lardellato

from Romeo Salta's

1 4-pound Fillet Mignon	2 wine glasses of red wine
1 tsp. salt	½ cup olive oil
¼ tsp. pepper	1 green onion, minced
5 slices Prosciutto ham (or Canadian bacon)	¼ tsp. rosemary
2 cloves garlic	

Use a prime or choice Fillet Mignon. Make three horizontal holes at the same distance apart. The holes should not go deeper than the center. Place some fresh Rosemary in one hole, two cloves of whole, peeled garlic in the center and minced onions in the third. Place five fatty slices of Prosciutto horizontally on both sides of the meat. Bind the meat together with thin white thread.

Place the meat in a heavy oven casserole with 1 pint of water and the olive oil. Place it in preheated oven set at 375 degrees. Turn the meat over every 15 minutes. At the end of the cooking time, pour the red wine over the meat and leave it in the oven for about 10 minutes.

Place the steak on a wooden board. Remove the thread. Salt and pepper to taste. Slice and pour over the remaining sauce.

Serves 6 to 8.

Costolette Di Vitello Al Cartoccio

(Veal Chops in Paper)

from Romeo Salta's

2 T. butter
¼ pound fresh
mushrooms, thinly
sliced
1 cup peeled, diced
tomatoes
2 slices prosciutto,
cut into strips
½ cup dry, white wine

2½ tsp. salt
½ tsp. freshly ground
black pepper
6 veal chops, cut
1-inch thick
3 T. olive oil
2 T. parsley, minced

Melt the butter in a saucepan. Saute the mushrooms 3 minutes. Add tomatoes, prosciutto, wine, 1 tsp. salt and half of the black pepper. Bring to a boil. Cook over low heat 10 minutes.

Season the chops with the remaining salt and pepper. Heat 2 tablespoons of oil in a skillet. Brown the chops on both sides. Cut 6 pieces of parchment paper or aluminum foil large enough to completely cover the chops. Brush with remaining oil. Place a chop in the center of each and cover with the sauce. Sprinkle with parsley. Fold over the paper, sealing the edges well. Place on a baking sheet.

Bake in a 375 degree oven for 15 minutes or until the chops are tender. Serve in the paper with the top rolled back.

Serves 6.

Romeo Salta's Paglia E Fieno Alla Papalina

(Straw and Hay for the Pope)

from Romeo Salta's

½ pound egg noodles (vermicelli)

½ pound spinach noodles (angel's hair or vermicelli)

¼ cup melted butter

1 clove garlic

1 cup prosciutto, thinly sliced

1 cup fresh or frozen peas

1 tsp. salt

1 pound mushrooms, sliced

½ cup clarified butter

2 cups bechamel sauce (prepared in advance)

1 cup Parmesan cheese

Cook pasta according to directions on package. Drain. Saute garlic in ¼ cup butter for 3 minutes. Discard garlic. Toss noodles with the garlic butter sauce. Set aside.

While pasta is cooking, saute mushrooms in heated butter for 8 to 10 minutes or until mushrooms have reabsorbed their liquid. Combine prosciutto, sauteed mushrooms , peas, salt and bechamel sauce. Simmer slowly over very low heat for 15 minutes.

Combine sauce with pasta, sprinkle with Parmesan cheese, and serve immediately.

Serves 6 to 8 people.

Chicken Scarpariello

from Romeo Salta's

2 3-pound chickens,
disjointed
2 T. olive oil
4 T. butter
2 tsp. salt
½ tsp. freshly ground
black pepper
1 clove garlic, minced

2 T. chopped chives or
green onions
¾ cup sliced mushrooms
1½ cups dry white wine
½ cup chicken broth
½ pound chicken livers,
cut in half
2 T. minced parsley

Have the chicken cut into small pieces, leaving the bone in. Wash and dry well. Heat the oil and 2 tablespoons butter in a deep skillet. Saute the chicken in the hot oil until it has browned. Sprinkle with salt and pepper.

Mix in the garlic and chives. Add the mushrooms, wine and broth. Bring to a boil and cook over medium heat 30 minutes or until chicken is tender.

Melt the remaining butter in a separate skillet. Saute the livers in it for 5 minutes or until very little pink remains. Season with a little salt and pepper. Add to the chicken and cook about 5 minutes. Sprinkle with parsley.

Serves 6 to 8.

149

Swiss Center Restaurants

Four thousand miles from home . . . but as authentic as dining in St. Moritz or Gstaad are the Swiss Center Restaurants on West 49th Street just off Fifth Avenue. When you dine here you'll discover that there is much more to Swiss cuisine than fondues . . . although this world famous old dish is of course still popular here.

To bring a bit of Switzerland to our city the restaurant has imported a team of eight native Swiss chefs who can provide a mouthwatering tour of their country. Swiss cuisine as it is prepared here combines the specialties of four cultures . . . German, French, Italian and Romansch. In Switzerland these four differing cultures have been co-existing for centuries. At the Swiss Center they make up a most interesting selection of dishes.

Two restaurants comprise the Swiss Center. The more formal Swiss Pavilion is a handsome contemporary dining room where bare walls are draped with flags representing the cantons of Switzerland. Downstairs at the Fondue Pot the atmosphere is casual and the prices somewhat lower. There is also an attractive bar and lounge area. The Bell Bar is where you can enjoy Swiss snacks with your cocktails amid a collection of huge hanging cowbells.

At the Swiss Pavilion you might begin dinner with Delice de Fromage Suisse . . . cheese croquettes topped with tomato sauce ($1.35) or escargots Vigneronnes . . . snails marinated in brandy, then baked in a butter sauce seasoned with 16 herbs and spices ($2.70). Ramequins . . . two small baked tartlets containing cheese and minced ham ($1.25) are also a popular choice.

There are several interesting soups on the menu such as Basler Mehlsuppe, beef stock blended with red wine, and zuppa ticinese, a beef boullion topped with toast, egg yolk and gruyere cheese that is browned under the broiler.

For your entree try the veal stuffed with ham and cheese ($9.50). It's excellent. So is the chicken breast filled with a blend of veal, nuts and honey, flamed with curacao and served with a fruit sauce ($9.00). There's also a good entrecote as well as the popular Swiss specialty Zurcher Geschnetzeltes . . . sliced veal and mushrooms in a cream sauce. Brook trout are kept in a tank from which you may select your own. Depending on your mood, it may be poached and served with Hollandaise sauce or boned and sauteed with grapes.

Naturally there is a wide assortment of fondues. The traditional fondue neuchateloise (made with Swiss and Gruyere cheese mixed with wine) and fondue au boeuf are the favorites. Cheese fondue can be traced back to the 18th century. Even Brillat-Savarin, the famed French gourmet, was enamoured by this dish. He was born in a French town close to the Swiss border and near the part of Switzerland where fondue is said to have originated. In his well known book, published in the 1880's, Savarin writes enthusiastically about fondue and is said to have created interest in this dish.

At the Swiss Center the Fondue Section of the menu enlightens us as to the background of eating this popular dish. According to the Swiss, sharing foods produces intrinsic relationships. There is no mention or evidence of the old Swiss custom of kissing your companion (of the opposite sex) should your bread drop off the fork while dunking it into the hot bubbling cheese. The couple dining next to us one evening were sharing fondue, but they were not adhering to custom. They were probably experienced fondue eaters or unaware of this old Swiss tale.

For dessert lovers, there's a tasty chocolate fondue served with a variety of fruits and cake for dipping. I found the origin of this dish a lot easier to trace. It had its beginnings in the 1960's when the Switzerland Cheese Association introduced the recipe as a way to create interest in one of Switzerland's most important milk products, chocolate.

Other interesting dessert offerings include a crepe stuffed with apple slices and raisins topped with a hazelnut sauce; open fruit tarts and dessert cheese from, of course, Switzerland.

It's downstairs at the Fondue Pot that you'll fine fondues you never imagined existed. The cheese fondues served here are enriched with tomatoes and oregano, with olives, anchovies and garlic or even bacon and tarragon. Raclette, another classic melted cheese dish is also on the menu.

Many of the same dishes that are served upstairs at the Swiss Pavilion cost a dollar or so less at the Fondue Pot. Here, too, is where the mood of Switzerland is enhanced by the enormous yodle suspended from the ceiling in the center of the room and the interesting old wooden farming tools and mountain climbing equipment. Outer iron shoes, axes, rope and whatever else one might need to climb the Matterhorn are hung attractively on the stucco walls amid scenes of this magmificent country.

At lunch in both restaurants the emphasis is on lighter entrees. Three fine quiches are offered . . . traditional cheese with bacon and onions; one with tomatoes, mushrooms and salami and a curry version with shrimp and shredded vegetables. Omelettes, a cold meat platter (which is very popular for lunch in Switzerland) and salads are also served.

Both restaurants are open for lunch from noon until 2:30 p.m. and dinner is served from 5 until 11 p.m. On weekends the Swiss Pavilion is open only on Saturday evening from 5 to 11 p.m., while the Fondue Pot is open both Saturday and Sunday from noon to 10 p.m. The Fondue Pot is busy at lunch and no reservations are accepted so you may have to wait for a table. Upstairs you can and should reserve a table.

The Fondue Pot also serves Sunday brunch. It's marvelous to stop here on a cold winter Sunday after ice skating across the street at Rockefeller Center. Of course it's not nearly as exhilarating as dining on Fondue after a morning on the ski slopes, but for those who are in the city on Sunday it is a lot of fun. You can warm up with a special brunch cocktail and then move on to enjoy crepes, an omelette or cheese dish prepared the Swiss way. Prices for brunch range from $2.50 to $4.50.

Speak to head chef Robert Keller if there is still a special dish that you enjoyed during your travels through Switzerland that you're longing to try again. A member of La Chaine des Rotisseurs, Chef Keller is charming, willing and able to prepare any dish provided you give him three days notice. Chef Keller has shared some of his recipes with us. Read them over and plan your own gastronomic journey through Switzerland. You will find the recipes not only simple to prepare and serve but delicious and fun to eat.

Croustade Oberland

(Swiss Rarebit)

from Swiss Center Restaurants

1 tsp. butter	1 T. white wine
1 T. flour	4 thin slices smoked ham
1 cup milk	4 slices natural Swiss or
salt, pepper, nutmeg	natural Gruyere cheese
to taste	4 slices white toast or
1 T. butter	2 English muffins
6 medium sized	
mushrooms, sliced	

Melt teaspoon of butter in a heavy saucepan. Add flour and stir until a golden color. Then remove from heat and slowly add milk, stirring well. Place over a low heat and continue to stir for 15 minutes. Season with salt pepper and nutmeg.

In another pan melt 1 T. butter and saute the sliced mushrooms. Add the wine and bring to a boil. Then add to sauce and simmer for 5 minutes.

Brown ham slices lightly in another pan. Now toast and butter bread and place in a heatproof serving dish. Cover with ham and mushrooms in sauce. Top with slices of cheese. Place on a cookie sheet and put in broiler for a few minutes until brown.

Garnish with a sprinkling of paprika.

Serves 2.

Fondue a la Paysanne

(a traditional fondue flavored with tarragon and bacon)

from Swiss Center Restaurants

½ lb. natural Swiss cheese, grated

½ lb. natural Gruyere cheese, grated

1 clove garlic

1½ cups dry white wine

1 T. lemon juice

1 T. cornstarch

3 T. Kirsch

1 T. tarragon, minced

6 slices crisp bacon, crumbled into small pieces

pepper to taste

2 loaves Italian or French bread cut into 1″ cubes with crust on one side.

Grate cheese. (You may do this in advance and refrigerate in a tightly closed plastic bag.)

Rub the inside of cooking pot (preferably earthenware or else enameled) with a clove of garlic that has been cut. Then discard garlic.

Add wine to pot and heat over a medium flame. When wine is hot but not boiling add lemon juice and grated cheese, stirring constantly with a wooden spoon until cheese is melted and mixture is smooth. Let it bubble; then add pepper and stir until blended. Mix cornstarch with Kirsch and add to the fondue, allowing it to boil for 15 to 30 seconds. Now add bacon and tarragon and mix well.

Remove pot from heat and place on a burner at the table and serve. Bread cubes should be speared with a long fondue fork through the soft side into the crust and swirled in the cheese.

Serves 4 as a main course; 24 as an Hor d'oeuvre.

Note: After the fondue is eaten a crust will have formed on the bottom of the pan. This can be lifted with a wooden spoon and served to guests for a delicious ending.

Fondue au Chocolat

from Swiss Center Restaurants

| 3 Toblerone milk choco- | ½ cup heavy cream |
| late bars, 3 oz. each | 2 T. brandy, rum or liqueur |

Break up chocolate into small pieces and place in the top of a double boiler. Add remaining ingredients and heat over a low flame. When chocolate is melted and mixture is smooth remove from heat and transfer to an earthenware fondue pot or chafing dish set over a candle or low flame.

Serve with sliced fruit (apples, oranges, bananas), strawberries, seedless grapes and bite size chunks of pound cake or anything else that you would like to dunk into the chocolate.

Serves 4.

Twenty One Club

In an elaborate brownstone on 52nd Street, the Twenty One Club proudly stands as one of the most distinctive restaurants in Manhattan. Filled with a million dollar art collection, a king's ransom in silver, a fantastically well-stocked larder, and one of the most incredible wine cellars in America, the Twenty One continues to be the "in" place to hang your hat in New York.

Opened by Jack Kriendler and Charlie Berns as a flamboyant speakeasy during Prohibition days, the Twenty One has most often been referred to as a fine, old dining club. It is a highly personal, family operated business, offering all the amenities of a lovely home or private club. The wonderful turn of the century charm lingers on from the days of its original owners and this landmark restaurant has always held great fascination for me . . . as well as its notable clientele of society first families, familiar faced politicians, Wall Street giants, and well-heeled patrons who enjoy the food and drink as much as I.

Enter the great restaurant . . . down a few steps and through the profusion of old black painted wrought iron, brought over from the original restaurant. Overhead is a battalion of colorful iron jockeys, each having once marked the famous stables of a high-ranking patron. It is impossible to get through the famous gates without a nod from Chuck Anderson, and if you are anyone special, a kiss from Jerry Berns! You have arrived, so enjoy yourself.

A comfortable paneled living room, flowing off to the right of the foyer, is charming with Remington paintings and inviting furniture. The television is going strong, and a delightful hustle and bustle begins as guests start wandering in for lunch.

Straight ahead is the bar. Go past the cigar counter, the cloakroom, the family and friends of the family and you will enjoy one of the most exciting "lunch breaks" around. Congregating around this massive mahogany standup bar, you might catch a glimpse of a Rockefeller or Ford. You might notice great conviviality, table-hopping, back-slapping and laughter. Veteran bartenders, immune to the crescendo of noise, are certain to pour you a well mixed drink.

While everyone is getting into the spirit of the day, Chef Anthony Pedrelli is busy in the kitchen, supervising a staff that numbers over a hundred. This kitchen prepares some of the city's great sophisticated American dishes, impressive with just the right amount of continental touches. Turbot is poaching in court bouillion, awaiting the exquisite mousseline sauce. At the same time, an All-American hamburger, selling for just under $6.00 is given the same tender care. Steak tartare, calves' liver and bay scallops are part of the large lunch menu, and lovely desserts, including an excellent chocolate mousse, are tranquil under mountains of whipped cream and meringue.

Though there are many tables crowded around the bar, unless you are a regular guest, you will probably be ushered to one of the three upstairs dining rooms. Dark stained paneling and heavy moldings, leather banquettes and elaborate silver trays on wooden wall shelves, cozy warmth and a lot of marvelous, elegant service surrounds you.

Lunchtime means a number of interesting dishes . . . you may order a tureen brimming with rich turtle soup, a crisp salad, herbed omelette, a tender steak sandwich or an entire meal. Flavor, color and texture blend well and an army of competent waiters move faster and faster as the tables fill to capacity.

Wine is an important part of any meal at the Twenty one Club, and there is enough history in that famous cellar to write a book about. Behind an enormous door, weighing a ton, stand rack upon rack of incredible and rare vintages, some of prohibition days, some earmarked for a future celebration, some stored for regular patrons, and some, carefully chosen for you and me!

No restaurant writer can do justice to this kitchen without mentioning their expertise with wild game. Partridge, Pheasant, Rock Cornish Game Hens and Guinea Hen are just a few of their specialties. Cornish Hen Alexas, a superb dish made flavorful with wine and white grapes, is a gourmet recipe they were kind enough to share for this book. Stuffed Quail a la 21 is another delicacy, baked with zucchini and carrots, and seasoned with a hint of tarragon.

No restaurant in the city caters more to its pampered regular guests than does the 21. Favorites have had their dinners rushed to their hospital room, other pets use the steam and massage rooms that the establishment has long provided, birthday cakes can be whipped up on a moment's notice, complete with seranade, and there is almost no limit as to what is done to pamper a special "somebody."

Old timers in New York remember many locations where they have patronized this noted restaurant. At one time they were located in the Village. Later, the family moved on to West 49th Street. In 1933, they took over the present location. Private parties have gathered in upstairs dining rooms and enjoyed this glorious hospitality until the early hours of the morning!

Though the 21 Club has grown to nearly a $5 million dollar a year business, with expansions into the import of fine foods and cigars, though the barbershop that was once a daily ritual for Manhattan's best groomed men is long gone, though the restaurant has had its ups and downs, the family is still together. It is a glowing tribute to them . . . Pete and Bob Kriendler, Jerry Berns and Sheldon Tannen . . . that their loyalty and devotion have perpetuated the work Jack and Charlie began . . . and that the Twenty One Club still attracts so many loyal fans from all over the world!

Creamed Spinach

from The Twenty One Club

2 pounds fresh spinach	1½ tsp. salt
1 cup heavy cream	⅛ tsp. pepper
2 T. butter or margarine	Dash of ground nutmeg

Trim stems and coarse ribs from the spinach. Wash leaves well. Place spinach in a large kettle with 1 teaspoon salt. Cover. (No need to add any water.) Steam 3 to 4 minutes, or just until leaves are wilted; drain well. Put spinach, half at a time, into container of electric blender. Whirl until pureed, adding a little cream, if needed.

Heat butter or margarine in large saucepan; add spinach, remaining ½ tsp. salt, pepper and nutmeg. Cook, stirring often and adding remaining cream, little by little (about 2 tablespoons at a time) until spinach is thick and creamy. (about 15 minutes)

Serves 4.

Escallope of Salmon "21"

from The Twenty One Club

1 3 pound salmon	½ cup olive oil
(Filet it and cut into	Salt
¼ inch slices·	Black pepper
½ cup white wine	¼ cup flour
½ cup white vinegar	Bay leaves
	3 T. butter

Place sliced salmon in pan. Marinate in the wine, vinegar, olive oil, bay leaves, and salt and pepper for 5 or 6 hours. Remove from the marinade.

Dip filets in flour and saute in butter over high flame. Remove from pan and place in platter. Spoon Dill Sauce over the salmon and serve.

Dill Sauce

from The Twenty One Club

½ cup sherry wine	1 cup chopped dill
2 cups cream sauce	(fresh)
1 cup heavy cream	

Boil cream sauce and heavy cream with wine. At the last minute, add fresh dill. Spoon over Escallope of Salmon "21".

Stuffed Quail a la "21"

from The Twenty One Club

8 quail, thawed
½ of a small zucchini
½ of a large rib of
    celery
1 medium carrot, peeled
½ medium yellow
    onion, minced
½ package (10 ounce
    size) frozen petits
    pois
1 large clove garlic,
    minced

1 tsp. tarragon
2 shallots, minced
Salt and freshly ground
    pepper
8 T. butter
4 T. vegetable or
    peanut oil
¼ cup Cognac
1 cup heavy cream
1 cup white grapes
    (about ½ pound)

Slice the zucchini, celery and carrot in long, thin strips. Then cut across into very small dice. Combine with the peas and garlic in a heavy saucepan. Add enough boiling water to cover. Bring to a boil and boil briskly for three minutes. Cool under cold running water. Drain. Mix with the shallots, tarragon and plenty of salt and pepper.

Dry the cavity of each bird with paper towels. Then, using a teaspoon, fill each cavity with the vegetable stuffing. Truss securely with fine white string. Sprinkle with salt and pepper. The quail can be prepared to this point ahead of time. If done early in the day, cover securely and refrigerate. Bring to room temperature before sauteeing.

Heat 4 T. of butter with 2 T. oil in each of two heavy skillets. Place four quail in each skillet and saute, using fairly high heat. Turn birds over and over until beautifully brown on all sides. (about 15 minutes) Do not overcook or the meat will be dry and tough.

Lift the cooked birds to a heated serving platter and keep warm. Pour off and discard all the fat from the two pans. Add the Cognac to one pan, place over a low heat and simmer, stirring to incorporate all the juices. Then add the cream and grapes. Increase heat and cook until the cream has thickened lightly. Season with salt and pepper. Pour over the quail.

Serves 4.

Sabayon with Strawberries

from The Twenty One Club

7 egg yolks	1 pint strawberries,
½ cup sugar	washed and hulled
1 cup Marsala or	
sherry wine	

Beat egg yolks and sugar slightly with wire whip or rotary beater in top of double boiler. Beat in Marsala. Place over simmering, not boiling, water. Cook, beating constantly at a steady beat, until the mixture thickens slightly and is double in volume. (about 20 to 25 minutes.) Remove top of double boiler from hot water. Keep beating a few minutes longer.

To serve: Pile strawberries high in serving bowl. Spoon part of sabayon sauce over berries. Serve remainder of the sauce in a small bowl.

Serves 4.

Cornish Hen Alexis

from The Twenty One Club

4 cornish hens	Salt and pepper
2 carrots	1 tsp. shallots, chopped
2 stalks celery	fine
1 onion	1 lemon
2 bay leaves	¼ cup white wine
Dash of rosemary	4 T. sour cream
¼ lb. melted butter	1½ cups white seedless
(1 stick)	grapes
1½ cups flour	Chopped parsley
1 quart chicken broth	Vegetable oil

Roast four cornish hens in a casserole at 350 degrees for 15 minutes, basting occasionally with vegetable oil. Then add (all diced) carrots, celery, onion, bay leaves, and rosemary.

Cook an additional 20 minutes, basting occasionally. When cooked, remove the birds and place aside. While birds roast, make a thick roux using the melted butter and flour. Add chicken broth which is hot gradually until the roux is a smooth, fairly thick mixture. Season with salt and pepper. For a smooth veloute, simmer 15 to 20 minutes.

While the veloute is cooking, saute in a separate pan a little butter, 1 tsp. shallots, the juice of one lemon, ¼ cup white wine and the sour cream. When hot, add to the chicken veloute.

Prior to serving, add white grapes to the veloute. Pour this over the cornish hen in casserole and heat again. Sprinkle with chopped parsley on each bird and serve.

Onion Soup Gratinee

from The Twenty One Club

2 T. Clarified Butter (see below)
2 large Bermuda onions, sliced
1½ tsp. flour
2 cans condensed chicken broth
1 1/3 cups water
1 tsp. salt
⅛ tsp. white pepper
4 slices French bread, toasted
4 T. grated Parmesan cheese

Heat clarified butter in large saucepan or dutch oven. Saute onions over medium heat, stirring often, until soft. (about 15 or 20 minutes.) Sprinkle flour over onions and stir in broth, water and salt and pepper. Heat to boiling stirring constantly. Lower heat and cover. Simmer 30 minutes.

Ladle soup into 4 individual fireproof soup bowls. Float a slice of toasted bread on each and sprinkle with Parmesan cheese. Broil about 4 inches from the heat until cheese turns golden brown.

Serves 4-6.

Clarified Butter

Melt 1 stick butter in top of double boiler over simmering water. Pour off clear liquid. Discard white sediment. Refrigerate clear liquid to use in recipes.

Index

169

FOWL

MEATS

SAUCES

SOUPS AND STOCKS

SWISS FAVORITES

VEGETABLES AND SALADS

Notes